No.
2. Representative American Speeches:
1950-1951. A. C. Baird. $1.75.

No.
6. Gambling in America. H. L. Marx,
Jr. $1.75.

Volume 22

No. 3. Representative American Speeches:
1949-1950. A. C. Baird. $1.75.

Volume 21

No. 2. Representative American Speeches:
1948-1949 A. C. Baird. $1.75.

Volume 20

No.
5. Federal World Government. J. E.
Johnsen. $1.50.

No.
6. Federal Information Controls in
Peacetime. R. E. Summers.
$1.50.

Volume 19

No. 3. Free Medical Care. C. A. Peters. $1.25.

Volume 18

No.
3. Representative American Speeches:
1944-1945. A. C. Baird. $1.25.
5. Anatomy of Racial Intolerance.
G. B. de Huszar. $1.25.

No.
6. Palestine: Jewish Homeland? J. E.
Johnsen. $1.25.

Volume 17

No. 4. Representative American Speeches:
1943-1944. A. C. Baird. $1.25

Volume 16

No.
1. Representative American Speeches:
1941-1942. A. C. Baird. $1.25.

No.
6. Representative American Speeches:
1942-1943. A. C. Baird. $1.25.

THE REFERENCE SHELF

Vol. 28   No. 5

THE GOVERNMENT
AND
THE FARMER

Edited by
WALTER M. DANIELS

THE H. W. WILSON COMPANY
NEW YORK   1956

PREFACE

This volume was prepared to provide material on the "problem area" designated by the National University Extension Association for high school discussion and debate in the academic year 1955-56. Its contents describe and suggest remedies for the ills besetting American agriculture.

An effort has been made to draw principally upon materials published since 1951. Discussion of farm problems up to that date was fully covered by a previous volume in this series: Robert E. Summers, *Subsidies for Farmers* (The Reference Shelf, Volume 22, Number 4).

The problems of the farmer and attempts by the Federal Government to deal with them are described in the first two sections of this book. Four succeeding sections take up the four principal issues in the debate: price supports, surpluses, acreage restrictions or "retirement," and the low-income family farm. In the final section, various economic research groups address themselves to remedial regimens for a sick farm economy.

The editor is grateful to the authors and publishers who have given their permission for reproduction of the materials quoted in this book.

WALTER M. DANIELS

July 3, 1956

CONTENTS

PAGE

PREFACE 3

I. WHY THE FARMER NEEDS HELP

Editor's Introduction 9

Hearst, James. Farmers Can't Do It Alone ....
.... Commonweal 9

What Ails Agriculture .... Business Week 13

Kramer, Dale. A Successful Farmer's Dilemma ....
.... Reporter 21

Jesness, O. B. No "Miracle Medicine" ....
.... Nation's Business 27

Fite, Gilbert C. Farm Policy, 1919-32 ....
.... Current History 30

Saloutos, Theodore. Farm Policy, 1933-39 ....
.... Current History 35

Warne, Colston. Farm Policy, 1940-52 ... Current History 38

The Brannan Farm Program .... Consumer Reports 41

II. PRESENT FEDERAL FARM POLICY

Editor's Introduction 46

Blair, William M. Glossary of Farm-Bill Terms ......
.... New York Times 46

Benson, Ezra Taft. Benson's Program, as He Sees It ....
.... Collier's 49

Brannan, Charles F. As Brannan Sees Benson's Program
.... Collier's 52

Benson, Ezra Taft.   Administration's Farm Program   55

Ellender, Allen J.   Senate Committee's Bill .. Facts Forum   58

Eisenhower, Dwight D.   President's Veto Message   62

Morris, John D.   Original and Revised Farm Bills Com-
    pared .... New York Times   67

III. PARITY AND PRICE SUPPORTS

Editor's Introduction   70

Henderson, Harry S. and others.   Current Price Support
    Activities   70

Bradley, Ralph S.   For High, Rigid Supports   76

Why the Farmer Needs Full Parity   78

Brandt, Karl.   Failure of Rigid Supports   81

Defects in Support Policies   84

Ogren, Kenneth E.   Where Your Food Dollars Go   88

IV. SURPLUSES

Editor's Introduction   93

Thruelsen, Richard.   Too Much Is Our Trouble ......
    .... Saturday Evening Post   93

Shepherd, Geoffrey S.   Can We Eat Up Our Surpluses? ...   100

Johnson, Glenn L.   Can We Feed Future Generations? ...   104

Expanding Domestic Consumption   105

Roe, Jim.   Selling the Farmer's Products ....
    .... Successful Farming   108

James, Ben.   Expanding Overseas Markets ....
    .... Nation's Business   111

Russell, J. Stuart.   Feeding the World Better ....
    .... Christian Century   114

Jesness, O. B.   Problems of Selling Abroad   116

V. ACREAGE "RETIREMENT" PROGRAMS

Editor's Introduction 122
Benson, Ezra Taft. The Administration's Program 122
What's This Soil Bank Idea? ....
.... U. S. News & World Report 126
Will Plan Help Those Who Should Be Helped? .. Fortune 129
Newsom, Herschel D. Views of the Grange 132
Views of American Farm Bureau Federation 133
Gehlbach, Melvin F. Views of Soil-Bank Association 135
Penn, Raymond J. and Loomer, C. W. Conservation as an
    Objective 139
Poirot, Paul L. A Farmer Challenges Controls 142

VI. FAMILY AND LOW-INCOME FARMS

Editor's Introduction 145
Benson, Ezra Taft. Our Rural "Underprivileged" .....
.... Current History 145
Fewer Farmers—Bigger Shares .... Business Week 150
Bird, John. Can the Family Farm Be Saved? ....
.... Country Gentleman 153

VII. SUGGESTED PROGRAMS

Editor's Introduction 158
The Lessons of the Past 159
Three Fundamental Problems 166
Five Deficiencies in Policies 170
What Policies Merit a Trial? 176

BIBLIOGRAPHY 184

I. WHY THE FARMER NEEDS HELP

EDITOR'S INTRODUCTION

What are the American farmer's problems, how did they arise, and why does he need the government's help? This section, in two parts, offers answers to these questions as a basis for discussion of present government farm policy and of specific phases of agriculture's ills.

The section opens with a discussion by a farmer-writer of the problems of the nation's producers of food and fibers. Economic aspects of the present crisis, with their impact on the over-all economy, are discussed by a business weekly. A typical dirt farmer tells what he is up against after ten years of "damned successful" operation. An agricultural economist cautions against wishful thinking that any "miracle medicine" can be found for all the farmer's aches and pains.

The second part of the section is devoted to the history of farm policy in this country since World War II. Three articles by historians cover periods between 1919 and the end of the New Deal and Fair Deal administrations. An analysis of the "Brannan Plan," the most controversial proposal of that era, is quoted from a consumer publication.

FARMERS CAN'T DO IT ALONE [1]

The farmers are complaining again. Mass meetings like those of the twenties and thirties are being held in the Midwest to protest falling farm prices and rising farm costs. . . . The boom is running smoothly for almost everyone else; employment is at high levels, wages and prices keep inching up, factories face full schedules, dividend payments are high. Why is the farmer headed the other way? Does he have a case?

[1] From "Case for the Farmer," by James Hearst, an Iowa farmer and writer for farm publications. *Commonweal.* 63:159-61. November 18, 1955. Reprinted by permission.

The city housewife who reads in the paper that farmers own
4.5 million automobiles can scarcely keep her voice down when
she prices steak at the supermarket. When her husband pays the
grocery bill, he is likely to wonder why he has to be taxed to
support farm prices when food costs are already out of sight.
If the farmers are that well off, he thinks, they hardly need help
from the Government. Perhaps it is time for the farmer to offer
his side of the story.

Three out of five people in the world's population go to bed
hungry every night. It is our great good luck in the United
States to live in a country which can feed us all and feed us
well. We not only eat well, but we eat the most expensive food,
the high-protein, high-sugar diets. This kind of diet is expensive
in terms of land resources. Dr. John Black, an economist at
Harvard, estimates that "An acre of Corn Belt land, planted to
corn, will grow enough calories of food energy to support two
or three people for a year. But it takes two acres of corn fed to
hogs to support one person for a year, two and a half if fed to
dairy cows, six if fed to laying hens, and twenty if fed to beef
cattle."

The people on the farm who produce this high-standard diet
grow smaller in number as their efficiency increases. One hundred years ago the work of five farm people fed themselves and
one person in the city. Today, four farm people feed themselves,
twelve people in the city and two in another country. This shift
illustrates graphically the effects of machine power, hybrid seeds,
fertilizer techniques and improved management of human and
soil resources. It also helps to explain the problem of surpluses.

The accumulation of more food and fiber than we can use is
one aspect of the farm problem, but only one. According to a
Federal Reserve Bank report of 1953, the people who derive
most of their income from working the land constitute about
15.5 per cent of the total population. But these farmers, even
with the addition of money received from Government price supports, are paid only 6 per cent of the national income. In terms
of income, although not of production or efficiency, agriculture
is a declining industry. In September 1955, *Business Conditions*
—a review issued by the Chicago branch of the Federal Reserve

Board—summed up the situation neatly: "The farm operator with his wagon deeply mired in surplus supplies," it said, "enviously watches the business boom roll by. After four years of continuous decline farm operators' net income is now running 27 per cent below its 1951 peak."

But why is agriculture a declining industry in terms of income? Why does the farmer enviously watch the boom roll by and not join the procession? Farm and Government economists can give better reasons for low farm prices than solutions for improving them. There are three main reasons why the farmer, at present, is marching against the parade of boom prices.

For one thing, the American farmer is at the mercy of forces, both man-made and natural, which are beyond his control. Like all producers of raw material, he is the victim of a kind of reverse business practice where he seems to sell at wholesale and buy at retail prices. When the food or fiber which he raises is first sold, it goes through a long series of processing and packaging operations before it reaches the final consumer. Consequently the farmer receives less than half of the dollar (about 47 cents) which the customer in a grocery store spends for his bread and butter.

But when he buys a tractor or commercial fertilizer, he buys from a local dealer at the full retail price. And the spread in price between what the farmer receives and the consumer pays is widening as people ask for more processing—instant oatmeal, for example, and special packaging which provides meat already cut, trimmed, and frozen for immediate use.

The farmer's chief virtue, which also seems to be his principal bugbear, is his dedication to full production. It is his business to grow things and the occupational risks of weather, insects, blight, markets and prices cannot be accurately predicted at the beginning of the season. Once the farmer has set the cycle of growth in motion, there is little he can do to change it until it has completed its course. This is why the flow of milk, meat and grain from the farms maintains a full current year after year.

The vagaries of weather make it difficult for him to adjust production to demand. It is not possible for the farmer to arrange sunshine, rain and frost in such a way that the nation has enough food to safeguard it against shortages, and yet not enough to depress prices. Furthermore, where food prices are concerned, a small increase in supply will make a large decrease in retail prices. A 6 per cent increase in butterfat over the normal demand might cause a 20 per cent drop in price. The violence of such fluctuations leaves the farmer somewhat bewildered and almost helpless.

This inability to control his production leaves the farmer bouncing on an erratic and unstable price level. In national emergencies he is well rewarded as prices shoot up and buyers flock to market. But in peace time, when the farmer loses his big customers, he becomes a poor relation, hat in hand, asking for help.

Tariff laws are based on the principle that if the general welfare requires it, certain interests are entitled to Government help and protection. With this principle in mind, the farmer felt justified in asking for a farm loan. He knew that aid was often extended to shipping and manufacturing interests when the general welfare was in question. If a subsidy is not "creeping socialism" when used to further some business interest, he decided, farming should be able to be protected in the same way.

The farmer bases his argument for Government assistance on his record of production—a record which does not rise and fall sharply from year to year. This assurance of enough food and fiber to supply the nation through good times and bad is a national asset of incalculable worth. In 1932, for example, the worst year of the depression, farm income declined from an index of 142 in 1929 to 59. But where industry closed down and waited for the storm to pass and industrial production declined from an index figure of 110 to 58, agricultural production dropped barely 3 per cent. A steady and dependable supply of food and clothing is one of the benefits the consumer receives for the taxes he pays in support of farm prices. He is entitled to know what his money is spent for and how much the farm program costs him. But the farmer would like to know how much it is worth to the customer to know that he will not go to bed hungry.

The people of the cities need food; the farmer needs above all else a stable price level, and most of the farm programs have been pointed toward that goal. . . .

The price of farm products is not, of course, set by the farmer. He must accept what the market will pay him, and consequently he is at the mercy of the forces that govern the market. Since small changes in production cause large shifts in price, he needs to have the peaks and valleys of prices somewhat leveled out. The citizen who helps support farm programs with his taxes is giving his assistance in this task.

Figures concerning the cost of the farm program have often been distorted. A late release by the United States Department of Agriculture shows that one hour of factory labor in 1929 would buy 1.2 pounds of steak; in 1954 it would buy 2 pounds. Seven and eight-tenths pints of milk equaled one hour of factory labor in 1929; in 1954 the amount was 16.2 pints. In other words, the city dweller is spending considerably less of his working time earning his food now than he did twenty-five years ago.

The benefits of the farm program are obvious enough. The actual dollar expenditures show what the program has cost the taxpayer. According to an official Department of Agriculture report, the net loss for the whole farm program, including price support expenditures, for the past twenty years is a little over $1 billion. As a comparison, this is about the same amount of money that is appropriated for aids and special services to business in one year.

WHAT AILS AGRICULTURE [2]

Here we are in the biggest boom ever, and it's almost axiomatic to say, "Everyone is getting his share except the farmer."

After one hundred years of being helped at public expense, the farmer still isn't satisfied. Doing something for the farmer has again become the hottest domestic political issue. . . .

For years, the farmer was told that the rest of the country could not prosper if he did not. Yet his income has been going

[2] From "What's Behind the New Farm Crisis." *Business Week*. p 106-26. December 10, 1955. Reprinted by permission.

down, while the rest of the economy rolls from one prosperity peak to another.

He has always believed that higher prices for his products furnished the one overriding solution to all his problems. But today farm leaders, and even some political leaders, are telling him that farm prices should be lowered.

He has believed that a large and stable population of farmers was necessary for national well-being. Now he is being told —and he's inclined to agree—that there are too many farmers.

He has always had faith in the ultimate political power of farmers. But now he realizes that his numbers are diminishing, his influence is weakening. . . .

As a result, more hard thinking is being done right now about the place of farming in modern life than at any time in the past two decades and more. There is sudden recognition that United States agriculture has changed radically over the past fifteen years, that new solutions are therefore necessary. . . .

The key year is 1940.

Trends that had slowly been gathering strength for years broke swiftly into new ground under the impact of war. . . . Over the past fifteen years, agriculture has experienced a breakthrough, mechanically and technologically. Output is now at heights undreamed of before 1940, and it is still rising.

During the war years there was a widely held hope that when peace came, the increase in population would take care of agricultural surpluses that had plagued the country during the depression of the 1930's; that in a new farming era the demand for food would outstrip the ability of farmers to produce. This was a serious misreading of the nature of American agriculture.

True, population has been going up even faster than expected. But since 1940 the rate of population gain has been somewhat less than 2 per cent a year—while farm production has been going up at more than 2 per cent a year.

Thus, population growth will not solve the problem of surpluses in the foreseeable future; the gap between production and consumption will actually widen unless some basic change is made in the economic organization of farming. This is the professional judgment of the long-range thinkers in the United

States Department of Agriculture, and the belief is being shared more and more by farmers themselves.

The fact that farmers can increasingly out-produce their market puts them at a basic disadvantage when it comes to trading their products for the output of the rest of the economy. Thus, since 1950, the prices of products farmers sell have been falling, and the prices of goods farmers buy have been rising.

Compared to 1947-49, prices received by farmers have dropped 7 per cent, while prices paid by farmers for supplies, interest, labor, and the like, have gone up 12 per cent. Net income to the farm population as a whole from strictly farming activities is therefore down sharply—from $11.7 billion per year in 1947-49, to $9.9 billion last year. This is a drop of 15 per cent. The decline is continuing this year; it is the chief factor in the rising clamor from farmers.

If this were the whole story, agriculture would be in the midst of an extremely acute depression. But it is not the whole story. It leaves out one of the most dramatic changes in agriculture since 1940—the speeding up of the flow of people out of farming. Farm people are leaving agriculture at a rate of 1 million a year. (This includes farm people of all kinds—nonworkers as well as workers.)

Despite the traditional excess of births over deaths among farm people, there has been a net drop of 27 per cent in the number of people on farms since 1940. The number of farms in the same period dropped 15 per cent. This does not mean that land is being taken out of production. It means that fewer farmers are operating larger farms.

Largely because a smaller number of farmers are dividing up income from the sale of farm products, the per capita income of farmers has held up much better than the income to farming as a whole. . . . Compared to 1951—an exceptionally good year for farmers because of Korean War demand—per capita income of farmers has dropped 7 per cent. . . .

Aside from price supports, farmers have been losing a succession of skirmishes in Washington.

The amount of farm income coming from Government payments for soil conservation has declined steadily. In 1940, conservation payments ran $550 million and accounted for 6 per cent of farmers' cash income. This year they are only $200 million, less than 1 per cent of cash income. . . .

Farm spokesmen have been demanding that commodity surpluses in Government hands be dumped abroad at cut-rate prices. This has been resisted successfully both in Congress and by the Administration. . . .

In another ten or fifteen years the ratio of farmers to the rest of the population will approach that of New England, where they are now 5 per cent of the total. . . .

"We have only a few years left to write a farm policy to suit ourselves," one veteran farm organization spokesman puts it. "After that, the rest of the people will be writing one for us."

In the meantime, forces within agriculture itself are changing its claims on public policy. The once solid farm bloc—welded into a unit during the depression years—is breaking up. Farmer is now competing against farmer for a favored place in the price-support law; this split is along commodity lines. It is also recognized that the troubles of commercial farmers differ sharply from the needs of subsistence farmers; this split is along income lines. . . .

One of the venerable political shell games in the United States is to cite the low average income of all "farmers" as proof that agriculture is in dire straits.

This is still done occasionally, but rarely any more by responsible spokesmen for either party. They have discovered—as business analysts of the farm market did some time ago—that there is a class of permanently poor farmers whose incomes are always low whether times are good or bad. By including these people in an average of all farm incomes, the level is dragged far below the real incomes of the farmers who produce for the market in important quantities. . . .

The 1954 United States farm census—results of which were announced . . . [recently]—gives a count of 4.8 million farms in the country. That's a drop from the 5.3 million in the previous count taken in 1949.

How do these 4.8 million farms divide by economic class?

One hundred thousand very large farms and ranches are in a group by themselves. They produce 25 per cent of all agricultural products; their average sales exceed $25,000 a year. Some of these are currently in trouble because of falling livestock prices. . . .

Two million fairly large family commercial farms produce about 60 per cent of total agricultural products. This group is so important it requires a closer look later.

One million or so small family farms produce about 8 per cent of the output. Some are in the process of climbing into the class above (the two million) by buying adjoining land. Some are too small even to start up the ladder.

[There are] 1.7 million units [which] are more nearly rural residences than farms. They are a miscellany. The operators of some 700,000 of these units work more than one hundred days a year at some other livelihood. This number is increasing rapidly. It includes many factory and white-collar workers, as well as businessmen who farm as a tax-deductible—or perhaps profitable—hobby. But none are full-time professional farmers. Another group of the 1.7 million produces practically nothing; these farm owners sell less than $250 a year worth of farm products each, and do not work much at other jobs, either. They include the retired and the ill.

It's in the last two classes that you find, at the bottom of the income scale, the one million farmers who are permanently poor because they lack the resources to be anything else. They are on farms that are too small to support a family at anything but a subsistence level. Most of them are in the South. Higher prices don't solve their problems—they don't produce enough for the market. . . .

There is now general recognition that low-income farmers comprise a social welfare problem apart from the problems of commercial farmers.

It is the great middle group of farmers—the two million who run the fairly large family commercial units—whose needs have always been looked after in farm legislation. They still have the power; they will largely shape the new farm program. . . .

Taking the past fifteen years as a whole, this group has done very well. Its members have liquid assets totaling about $19 billion, and their debts of all kinds probably do not exceed $18 billion. The price of their land is going up steadily, despite the drop in commodity prices.

They are investing heavily in new machinery and equipment. Tractor output the third quarter of this year was almost 30 per cent above the same period last year; other farm equipment was up 15 per cent.

Materials handling equipment, pipeline milkers on dairy farms, and crop-drying units to improve storage efficiency are moving briskly.

The drive of these farmers for greater production with less labor is what broke farming out of its pre-1940 pace. There is every sign that they are pushing as hard as ever.

So far, increased productivity has kept this group ahead of falling prices. In 1949, farmers produced $15 worth of corn to the acre; now they produce $53 worth. Wheat has jumped from a $10 output per acre to $38, and cotton from $20 to $113 per acre. Some of this rise is due to higher prices, of course. . . .

Economists at midwestern agricultural colleges are advising farmers that corn should be back to $1.20 per bushel next year, that hogs will advance in price correspondingly, and that the outlook is fairly stable for cattle. . . .

But the 2 million will still have a serious complaint. Their average level of income has either declined or remained static for the past several years while incomes of people in other callings has been rising. This is what they are thinking about when they criticize the wage gains made by union labor and the higher profits of business. Over most of the past decade and a half, up to the last few years, they have gained greatly; they have no intention now of staying placidly on the sidelines, watching the rest of the economy go past them.

The Crux of the Problem

Even if prices recover somewhat, the underlying problem facing the 2 million efficient family farms will remain.

Boiled down, the problem is overproduction of three key products—wheat, cotton, and corn. . . . Farm spokesmen sometimes say there is overproduction of all farm products, but this is a loose generalization.

In dollar value, more than half the farm products are produced, distributed, and consumed without government price supports, and therefore without any possibility of piling up into surpluses such as plague the three troublesome crops. The price of these nonsupported crops sometimes falls painfully low, as did hogs this autumn. But farmers know the drop is due to a 9 per cent rise in production; normally they will correct this sort of short-range overproduction in the next crop year.

Wheat, cotton, and corn, however, present a more difficult problem. There are simply too many resources devoted to these crops in the light of demand.

Under the price-support umbrella . . . production stays markedly in excess of what will be used. The excess has been piling up in Government surpluses and the Commodity Credit Corporation's holdings are rising to a level that is becoming hard for farmers to defend politically. . . .

By every measurement, wheat growers are in the worst jam, even after cutting down 25 million acres from the postwar peak. If they maintain prices at present levels, they would have to cut another 15 million acres out of production before they hit a balance with consumption. If they are willing to take a sharp price cut, however, the reduction in acreage would be less; some additional output might move into export, and some would be fed to livestock in competition with corn and the other feed grains.

However, there is probably not a complete solution in this direction. Every wheat producing country the world around has a surplus, and export competition will be fierce. Corn producers would fight vigorously. . . .

Farmers are debating policy with great energy but at cross purposes. . . .

The most heat is coming from a new group, the National Farm Organization; its leaders claim that thirty thousand members have rallied to their cause since they got started some six weeks ago. A respected veteran of farm protest movements of the 1920's and the 1930's—seventy-eight-year-old Dan Turner of Corning, Iowa—is the driving force.

Turner is a Republican; he was governor of Iowa in the early years of the depression, and was vice chairman of the Eisenhower campaign committee in the state in 1952. But he's calling for a revival of high price supports as the cure for farming ills. . . .

"Don't beg for crumbs," Turner tells his audiences. "Stand up and fight." The fight, he insists, should be for at least 90 per cent rigid price supports; he even mentioned 100 per cent.

Turner's solution—higher Government price supports—is still the only one that makes sense to many farmers. If prices go down again next year as much as they have this year his National Farm Organization could become a major force. But so far it appeals mostly to farmers in particular circumstances. . . .

The old, long-established Farmers Union is also demanding a return to 90 per cent or even higher price supports as the cure. . . .

Against Turner and the Farmers Union are ranged farm leaders of a different type. E. Howard Hill, forty-seven-year-old president of the Iowa Farm Bureau, is one of the most effective. . . .

Hill is a livestock farmer, and an agriculture graduate of Iowa State College. . . . He, too, has been peppering the Administration. But his target has been Secretary Benson, and his goal has been not higher price supports, but advancement of a plan known to farmers as the "soil bank" or the "fertility reserve". . . .

Essentially, these ideas . . . include the retirement of land from crop use. [For further details, see Section V, below, Acreage "Retirement" Programs.]

The land retirement plans all involve payments by the Government to farmers. Some advocate outright purchase of marginal crop land, to be leased or resold to farmers who agree to use it for grazing purposes only. Some favor a system of leasing entire farms to the Government, which would then withhold the land from cultivation. The soil bank proposal as such involves the leasing of parts of farms to the Government on a rotating basis in order to build up fertility.

There's nothing new in the basic concept. It was suggested early in the New Deal by Henry Wallace, for example. What is new is its acceptance today by large numbers of farm leaders, and by farmers themselves. . . .

Land retirement is gaining adherents among processors of some farm products, mainly flour millers. Some believe that a rental of $10 an acre would be sufficient to take the poorest 15 million wheat acres out of production. If farmers were offered this rental over a five-year period as a means of financing a switch into ranching or feed production, the total cost to taxpayers would be $750 million. In return, taxpayers would have a wheat economy adjusted to current demand, without further need for costly price-support activities.

There are many doubts about how such plans would actually work, of course. Enforcement of rental agreements could be a grave problem. Rental of parts of farms would reduce some to uneconomic size. Stripping down resources in the amount foreseen for wheat would have a damaging effect on many small towns in the Great Plains area. Such questions could quickly strip land retirement of its present political glamor. . . .

There are many signs that over the longer run, farmers themselves will force Congress to face the issue of too much land and too many people producing some crops. When this adjustment is finally made, the two million efficient family farmers may again resume the economic advance they believe is their due.

A SUCCESSFUL FARMER'S DILEMMA [3]

Herb Ring is a stocky, quick-moving man of thirty-eight who farms two hundred acres in Iowa. He is spoken of as a "damn good farmer" to distinguish him from simply a good farmer, and he has grown accustomed to think of himself as a success. . . .

[3] From "200 Acres in Iowa: 'We Need Help Right Now,' " article by Dale Kramer, author of *The Wild Jackasses*, a study of agrarian tides scheduled for fall 1956 publication. *Reporter*. 14:34-7. February 9, 1956. Reprinted by permission.

Herb came back from the Army late in 1945. Already he was a family man, for he and Evelyn, a neighbor girl, had seen no use in waiting until after the war to marry. Herb's older brother had taken over the home place, but . . . Herb's father, on retiring, had been careful to make an even division of assistance among his three children. Herb's share was $7,000. He had $2,000 of his own in the bank, accumulated from prewar savings, the sale of his car before going into service, and what he put aside from his sergeant's pay. Evelyn, living with her parents, had saved $900 from his allotment. So they had a total of nearly $10,000.

A 160-acre farm about ten miles from the Ring home place came up for sale, and Herb, wanting to get in a 1946 crop, bought it in a competitive market. Yet the price of $250 an acre was not considered unreasonable. The six-room house and the outbuildings were in good repair. Herb put down $6,000 and an insurance company lent him the $34,000 balance on a twenty-year mortgage at 5 per cent. This meant that he would have to get up $3,400 in principal and interest at the end of the first year.

Herb figured up . . . the new machinery he wanted would cost him . . . more than $6,000. Of course he couldn't afford it, and anyhow not much new equipment was available in the restricted post-war market. Second-hand machinery was high. He paid $800 for an eight-year-old tractor that had cost $1,100 new. He got a three-plow attachment for $200, a set of harrows for $100, disks for $125, and a couple of wagons at $90 apiece. Altogether he put $1,900 into second-hand essentials. He would borrow his brother's oats combine, his mechanical corn-picker and his hay baler. Or, if they should both need the equipment at the same time, he would hire a custom harvester.

The house would have to wait for new furnishings. . . . A car was a big item in the short market. Herb had to pay $700 for a 1940 Chevrolet that had cost little more than that when it was new.

All told Herb had spent $9,000 of his capital, and there still wasn't a live thing on the place. The cost of putting in a crop had to be met, and there was the cost of operating beyond that.

Therefore Herb went after another $5,000 of credit—and got it at the local bank on his note. His security was a second mortgage on the farm, a mortgage on his chattels, and—quite an important item—his father's signature. He paid $100 apiece for thirty brood sows. He gave $375 for three milk cows. Evelyn got three dozen hens from her mother and bought two hundred brood chicks at the hatchery. . . .

Herb spread lime on forty of the sixty acres he was putting into corn—the major Iowa cash crop, whether marketed directly or fed into pork and beef—but any real soil-building program would have to wait. For seed, tractor fuel, hired help, and other cash operating expenses he set aside $2,000. He would still need some credit for feed, hog vitamins, veterinarians' bills, and the like. Evelyn, who is strong if rather slight, put in a big garden. The weekly check for butterfat and eggs paid most of the grocery bill.

Twenty years earlier Herb would have needed the help of a full-time hand to farm the 160 acres. But now, working the tractor all day and part of the night, and with Evelyn doing nearly all the milking, he got by with only $400 in hired labor. The crop year was a good one. The corn averaged sixty bushels to the acre. He saved an average of nearly seven pigs from each of his sows.

Herb was in the Government corn program, and he took a loan on most of his corn, getting $4,500 of badly needed capital. After saving twenty of the best young sows from the hog crop, he marketed the balance at an average of $24.15 a hundredweight. His check was for $6,375. . . .

Herb figured $45 a week combined wages for himself and Evelyn. His net profit that first year was $2,800. Most of the gross cash income had gone to pay off the bank note and other operating indebtedness. Yet even the net-profit figure was a bit deceptive. He hadn't paid himself interest on his $10,000 investment. And of course there was $3,400 principal and interest to pay on the farm mortgage. When that was subtracted from $5,140—the total of net profit plus family labor—he could see why they had been forced to skimp on their living.

Of course Herb had to borrow again at the bank for his operating expenses. And wanting to get a better return for his corn, he plunged heavily on beef cattle for fattening. In May 1947, he got some relief by the sale of his fall hog crop. In Iowa hogs are traditionally known as "mortgage lifters." Herb was able to lift his chattel mortgage from everything except the beef cattle, which were for the time being living inexpensively on pasture.

In the fall of 1947, the second year, Herb and Evelyn relaxed. The corn was fine. Prices were rising. Herb was mastering the new farming methods that had been developed under pressure from the Government to increase wartime food production. The vitamins and minerals and special seeds were expensive, but Herb was convinced they paid dividends. His cattle and hogs hit top grades. That winter of his second year his checks totaled a fancy $17,000.

Yet he was able to figure only $3,150 as net profit. For one thing, the repair bills on the old machinery had been high. And the prices of all the things he had to buy were skyrocketing. It had been another year of skimpy living.

Herb realized that to afford the new machinery he wanted he would have to find more land so that he could put the equipment to maximum use. Fortunately he was able to rent forty acres nearby, and, feeling confident, he spread himself for the first time since coming home from the army. The major items were a tractor at $1,700, a combine at $2,000 and a cornpicker at $1,500. With other smaller items the total came to $8,000. He borrowed most of the money. . . .

In 1949 prices were on the rise again. Herb's net profit went above $4,000 for the first time. He bought a new Chevrolet—on terms—and Evelyn lavished $1,000 on new furniture. The next year they had a new baby and painted the house and barn and barnyard fences.

Then came the Korean War and soaring prices. Yet Herb's net profits for 1950 and 1951 did not rise very much. Costs had shot up too fast. He noticed that according to Iowa State College statisticians the cost of machinery and power had increased 400 per cent since 1940. Herb's own figures showed a doubling of operating costs since 1946. He tried to be cautious in buying new machinery, yet he always found himself paying interest on $4,000 or $5,000 of equipment mortgages. . . .

At the beginning of 1955, Herb, while feeling that nine years of hard work ought to have put him farther ahead, was not worried. He could look with satisfaction at the reduction of his farm mortgage by $15,300, down to $18,700. The interest load was lighter now. His implement notes were under $4,000. But his standard of living was not really very high. The car was going on six years old. Except for a television set, they had bought no important item for the house in five years. From year to year they had put off installation of running water. They ought to paint again. And the eight-year-old tractor was about due to be traded in for a new one.

When the price of hogs, the mortgage lifters, began to slide in the spring, Herb began to worry. In May he sold his fall crop at $17 a hundredweight, or 80 per cent of parity. [See "Glossary of Farm-Bill Terms," Section II, below.] That was going to pull down his net profit.

Then it happened. Hog prices began to spin dizzily to one new depth after another. Down they went to fourteen-year lows, down at last to 55 per cent of parity. Cattle prices sagged.

"I came out about even on my beef," Herb says. "The hogs killed me. I could have stood for $18. What I got was under $11. There on the hogs is the way I figured my loss for the year—somewhere close to $4,000."

When Herb says he "lost" $4,000, he doesn't mean his books will show a red figure that large. What has happened is that his usual net profit is wiped out and he and Evelyn have had their joint wages cut from $45 to about $20 a week. And of course he has gained nothing on his investment of some $30,000.

The harsh question staring Herb in the face is this: Where is the money for amortization and interest on his farm mortgage to come from? His 1956 total is $2,635. Heretofore the money had come out of his net profit—with an occasional chunk of his wages thrown in.

Herb isn't broke. Far from it. But he is frankly scared. He wrote to his farm-mortgage holder, asking if he might forgo the $1,700 principal this year, paying only the interest. So far there has been no reply. This is not surprising. There are many thousands of Herb Rings, and the insurance companies and other big investors have a major decision to make on the leniency of their credit policies.

If necessary, Herb can pay the $1,700. He can refinance his mortgage through the Federal Land Bank, clapping a bigger mortgage on the farm. In effect this would be digging into his savings. Many have already done it.

So Herb will still be in business this year. The bank will probably let him have all the operational credit he needs. But he won't buy the new tractor, or replace the 1949 Chevrolet, or paint the house.

According to Herb, he literally trembles when looking at his fixed costs. Land taxes have almost doubled since 1946. In the old days of live horsepower a man could trim expenses in a hurry. Nowadays costs are still mounting. Tractor fuel, repairs and hired labor will be higher. About the only place to cut is in the standard of living.

Herb is sore. "Evelyn and I have worked like dogs," he says. "Instead of going ahead, "I've gone back at least a year. That means I've really lost two years. If the market stays down and the price of land drops—why, three or four years will bust me flat." . . .

All evidence indicates that Iowa farmers want production payments. They want prices pegged, with the Government making up the difference between the market and the pegged figure. Such a program, they freely admit, is open Government subsidization. They argue that other elements of the economy, especially industry, are subsidized. They point to billions spent for armaments and declare that food is every bit as important as weapons. The cry of "regimentation" is seldom raised any more. Most are willing to accept production controls along with payments. . . .

In early January, the National Farm Organization roared into Herb Ring's county. On three days' notice eight hundred farmers packed a hall in Sigourney to hear Dan Turner. Five days later 1,005 members—half the farmers of the county— had been enrolled. Only a few of those approached failed to join, and the leaders expect to enroll more than 90 per cent of the farm population. [See the preceding article in this section, "What Ails Agriculture," for a discussion of the National Farm Organization and its leader, Dan Turner, a former governor of Iowa—Ed.] . . .

It can be seen from the example of Herb Ring and his neighbors that the current of protest in the Middle West does not come from poverty. But it is also untrue, as is often charged, that farmers are merely angry over failing to share in the national boom prosperity. They have been hurt. The young men are badly scared. And the older men are concerned with more than investment depreciation and the prospect of working for nothing. They are worried, as Herb Ring is, over the future of their children.

NO "MIRACLE MEDICINE" [4]

If agriculture were up against a single simple problem we would be justified in seeking a single simple solution. But the problems are legion.

Of pressing concern at the moment is what to do with the surplus stocks which have been built up by the price support program. Although the Congress authorized a "commodity set-aside" up to $2.5 billion to take care of surpluses, this action does not cause them to vanish into thin air.

Some observers argue that we should get rid of surpluses before we lower any supports. If we did this, however, it is not unlikely that the same people would next contend that the need to lower supports would no longer exist. And if this approach should prevail, we would then go merrily to work again rebuilding our surplus stocks—not an inviting prospect.

[4] From "There's No Miracle Medicine for Farm Ills," article by O. B. Jesness, head of Department of Agricultural Economics, Institute of Agriculture, University of Minnesota. *Nation's Business*. 43:56-8. January 1955. Copyright, 1955. Reprinted from the January issue of *Nation's Business*.

Another easy out, often advocated, is to expand our food consumption. But just how easy is this in a country as well fed as our own?

Nor is it as simple as it sounds to move our food surpluses to undernourished peoples beyond our borders. It is very difficult to earmark and to transport vast quantities of grain or butter and the like without disrupting our own market patterns and those of other countries. . . .

Yet our experience with the International Wheat Agreement, which the United States signed, together with several other nations to stabilize the world wheat market, indicates that . . . international arrangements provide no easy answer.

Contrary to popular belief, farm surpluses are not the result of reduced demand. They result instead from abundant production. And they are also specific, not general, in nature. To grasp their significance, we have to look at individual commodities, among which wheat is today our most pressing problem.

We immensely expanded our wheat acreage during World War II and in the immediate postwar years to meet the rest of the world's needs. We exported wheat in large volume to Western Europe, for example, because its fields were devastated by battle, and because our dollars, under the Marshall Plan and other foreign aid programs, enabled Western Europe to buy from us. Now, however, Western Europe has not only recovered but even increased its wheat-growing capacity. Other exporting nations also have more than ample stocks. There is not a market in sight to which we can sell all the wheat we stand ready to produce unless we want to subsidize impoverished "have-not" countries with funds with which they can purchase it from us.

If this were only a temporary situation and if all wheat were alike, market quotas and acreage restrictions, applied across the board, would be the answer. But what we require is a longer-run adjustment, fitted to each class of wheat. Lower prices will encourage some farmers to shift from wheat growing to something else. Certainly lower prices will increase the use of wheat for livestock feed, and make it easier to export. . . .

While cotton is not in as tough a spot as wheat, some adjustments will have to be made here with special emphasis on developing nonagricultural job opportunities for workers released from cotton growing.

Butter reflects a considerable shift in consumer requirements and preferences. The decline in bread eating has meant less table spread. At the same time margarine has been gaining decidedly in its race with butter and to raise butter prices by restoring 90 per cent supports will handicap it in that race.

Elsewhere in the dairy province we find that the supply of cheese is definitely ample, while a growing population daily enlarges milk consumption which is further helped along by some decline in prices.

Although dairy products have their troubles, they are not comparatively anywhere near as difficult as those plaguing wheat.

The cattle outlook, from the view of the stockman, is more promising for 1955. Prices dipped sharply in the fall of 1952 and in early 1953 when a lush market elicited the response of overproduction—a typical cycle situation which illustrates the tenacity of the supply and demand equation. However, as the number of cattle being raised keeps going down, as at present, prices will correspondingly go up. The number of hogs still appears to be on the upswing. Poultry and eggs which were also "overproduced" in response to earlier attractive prices, can be expected to show some downward adjustment in production in the months ahead.

Since price supports are not in effect on these products, the farmers who produce them depend for their prosperity upon their ability to assess the price, diet and related trends that are in the free competitive market.

Recently Secretary Benson has been under fire by some critics who seem to be pained by any reference both to the farm-to-city movement of population and to the increasing size of farms. The Secretary is charged with wanting to get farmers, especially small farmers, out of agriculture. Such critics forget that the movement of people toward the city has gone on since colonial days.

The net effect of this change from the rural to the urban has been to lift farm productivity (70 per cent since 1939) with the result that levels of living have been raised for both the farm and nonfarm segments of our population.

Those who profess to fear that our farms are becoming too big have as yet to prove that the individual farm unit is on the way out. Actually, we should focus our attention on how to increase the size of units which are too small to provide enough income for good family living, rather than to be troubled about farms getting too big. It will be a very long time, if ever, before the Department of Agriculture will have to worry about bigness in farming in the way that the Justice Department's antitrust division has to worry about bigness in business.

FARM POLICY, 1919-32 [5]

Agriculture's immediate difficulties in the post World War I period can be traced to high production, stimulated during the war, and declining export markets for several basic crops. In 1919, agricultural exports totaled $4,107,158,753, but by 1922 they had fallen more than 50 per cent to only $1,883,315,000.

As they recovered from wartime handicaps, foreign countries encouraged farm production at home and took less from the United States. . . .

The output of American farms was simply more than could be absorbed at profitable prices. Furthermore, a gradual change was occurring in dietary habits reducing the per capita consumption of some commodities. For example, people tended to eat less bread and more fruit and vegetables.

Moreover, tractor power freed millions of acres for commercial crop production which were no longer needed for oats or other horse feed.

Thus with heavy output, contracting foreign markets, the absence of Government price supports after 1919, foreign competition, and the general deflationary movement, United States farmers slumped into the depression. . . .

[5] From "Equality for the Farmer," article by Gilbert C. Fite, professor of history, University of Oklahoma. Current History. 26:91-8. February 1954. Reprinted by permission.

The agricultural depression was world-wide. Furthermore, the depression hit other industries as well as agriculture. But the farm situation was different because "agricultural prices fell first, fell fastest, and fell farthest."

As a result, farmers dropped into a position of serious disparity with industrial groups. . . .

Holding companies, mergers and other types of combinations had been formed by business and industry to stabilize and fix prices.

Labor had organized and gained some of the advantages which came from combination and cooperation.

But farmers were still functioning on an individual basis, competing with one another and with millions of farmers in other parts of the world. In the 1920's, however, farmers began to awaken to the reality of their disadvantageous position in the American economy.

Although many people felt that farmers must work out their own salvation, either individually or cooperatively, a growing number of farmers, farm leaders, and politicians insisted that the Federal Government must directly aid agriculture.

Several price-fixing bills were introduced in Congress in 1921. Probably only a relatively small proportion of farmers favored this type of Federal relief in the early 1920's, but the hard core of agricultural thinking between 1920 and 1932 was the growing demand that the Government adopt some system to assure fair prices to producers of basic farm commodities.

The main struggle was between those who would rely on help from Washington and those who believed farmers could, for the most part, solve their own problems. . . .

In May 1921, a bipartisan farm bloc was formed in Congress to press for legislative relief. . . .

Congress did pass several bills between 1921 and 1923 which were of interest and limited help to farmers. . . .

Such legislation might have certain long-range benefits, but many farmers and their leaders wanted a program which would directly raise farm prices. No relief was of fundamental importance, they argued, unless it restored the purchasing power of the farm dollar to its prewar level. . . .

George N. Peek, President of the Moline Plow Company, and Hugh S. Johnson . . . developed a plan of "equality for agriculture." Their scheme was incorporated in the McNary-Haugen bills, the most celebrated farm relief proposal of the 1920's.

The phrase "equality for agriculture" which they popularized became the battle cry of the farm crusade until the Agricultural Adjustment Act was passed in May 1933. Here was the idea of farm parity which finally became an accepted part of American farm policy.

Peek and Johnson saw the farmer's trouble in the operation of the protective tariff. They pointed out that agricultural tariffs did not protect farm crops of which the United States produced a surplus because the surplus forced the home market down to approximately world levels.

But while producers of surplus farm commodities had to take world prices, they were required to buy manufactured goods in a protected market where industrial tariffs were effective in maintaining higher prices.

In other words, farmers were buying in a protected market and selling in the competitive markets of the world.

The tariff principle must be amended, they said, so "it will do for agriculture what it does for industry." . . .

Surpluses were the burdensome factor. If they could be eliminated from the domestic market, then the price of farm commodities might rise behind a tariff wall. . . .

To remove surplus crops, Peek and Johnson proposed to dump them abroad at the world price. They were familiar with two-price sales tactics in industry, a policy which made it possible to produce in excess of domestic requirements, yet preserve higher prices at home. . . .

The McNary-Haugen bill was basically a marketing device. It was built on the philosophy that farmers could be helped if they were forced to participate in a great pool or cooperative enterprise. . . .

The . . . proposal was defeated in the House by a vote of 223 to 155. It was opposed by most business and industrial interests which feared higher food and raw material prices; by the

Coolidge Administration which maintained that the Government had no business buying and selling farm commodities; by many powerful Democrats who opposed extending the principle of protection; by the metropolitan press, and by some important agricultural leaders. . . .

The situation in 1925 on the development of Federal agricultural policy was a stalemate between Administration supporters of cooperative marketing, and the McNary-Haugenites who favored price-lifting legislation. . . .

Under pressure of one of the largest crops on record, the price of cotton dropped to ruinous levels in the early fall of 1926. Now southern congressmen and senators added their support to a revised McNary-Haugen bill.

With a combination of southern and western votes, it passed Congress in February 1927. President Coolidge, however, still thought it inadvisable for the Government to tinker with agricultural prices. He gave the bill a stinging veto. . . .

Congress was prompted to repass a revised McNary-Haugen measure in May 1928.

Again President Coolidge vetoed it. Although he cited a number of economic arguments against the bill, he objected to it principally on the grounds that it was "repugnant to the spirit of our institutions, both political and commercial." . . .

But the campaign between 1924 and 1928 to raise farm prices by Government action, and to give agriculture economic equality with industry and labor had accomplished more than was apparent in 1928.

The idea of ratio prices or parity had been popularized, a concept which formed the basis of succeeding legislation. Farmers also had been impressed with the need of compulsory cooperation. . . .

The Hoover farm program was incorporated in the Agricultural Marketing Act passed in June 1929. The new law was designed to aid and stimulate cooperative marketing, to deal with seasonal surpluses, and to stabilize farm prices. . . .

The principal emphasis was on orderly marketing and stabilizing prices, not on obtaining definite price increases. . . .

As farm surpluses piled up, Hoover and other high Administration officials urged farmers to cut their production voluntarily. This advice was sullenly ignored. Besides finding it difficult, farmers disliked the economics of scarcity. . . .

Thus the idea grew that farmers must be given some positive enticement to restrict output.

The result of this thinking was growing support for the domestic allotment plan. . . .

Farmers were to be given a domestic allotment which was the amount of their production which they could sell for domestic use. On that portion they were to be given allotment certificates, roughly equal to the amount of the tariff, which processors would have to buy before they could move a commodity into domestic consumption. . . .

When producers became keenly aware of the price differential between the part of their crop used at home and that sold abroad, it was hoped they would cease producing the low-price surplus. . . .

Here was a basic shift of emphasis in agricultural policy-making, and one which most farmers and farm leaders bitterly opposed. Nonetheless, they came reluctantly to support the plan's basic principles because of the desperate condition of the entire farm industry.

Yet their fight for economic equality between 1920 and 1932 was of great importance. It was a significant turning point in the history of American agricultural policy. . . .

This period is the major dividing line between the traditional individualism and self-reliance of American farmers, and their acceptance of and demand for positive Government help in solving their problems.

The Agricultural Adjustment Act passed in 1933 was not the work of fuzzy-minded idealists or impractical college professors. Behind it was over ten years of agitation by highly organized pressure groups which demanded some form of Government aid for farmers.

FARM POLICY, 1933-39 [6]

The first Agricultural Adjustment Act became law on May 12, 1933. Its stated over-all objective was to restore the purchasing power of the farmers. This was to be accomplished by limiting the production of certain basic commodities, the curtailment of which was expected to influence the prices of other commodities and lead the way to recovery. . . .

A prime purpose of the AAA was to furnish the farmer with a parity price. For most products a parity price was defined as one that gave the producer a purchasing power equivalent to that which he enjoyed during the base period, usually from August 1909, to July 1914. . . .

The years from 1909 to 1914 were selected as the "parity" period because these years were considered ones of "balanced production on farms and [because] agriculture was in good balance with the rest of the nation." . . .

Passage of the AAA committed the Federal Government to practices it had never engaged in previously. The Government, instead of encouraging the farmer to become a more efficient producer, and providing him with credit and marketing facilities to achieve this end, assumed responsibility for raising his purchasing power to levels he knew from 1909 to 1914.

The agricultural program was a part of a much broader one calculated to aid the entire economy [National Industrial Recovery Act]. But the feeling prevailed that agriculture was in a disadvantageous position, and that consequently special action had to be taken to raise it to a status of equality with the other sectors of the American economy.

The role of the Federal Government changed from one of an advisory capacity to that of planning and adopting positive measures to facilitate the recovery of farming.

Production controls were the most novel portions of the New Deal farm program. Farmer organizations had agitated for such

[6] From "The Farmer's New Deal," by Theodore Saloutos, associate professor of history, University of California at Los Angeles. *Current History.* 26:99-104. February 1954. Reprinted by permission.

controls at a much earlier time, but their pleas went unheeded. Neither farmers nor legislators were prepared to accept such drastic recommendations. . . .

Farmers who received benefit payments and commodity loans had to comply with the control program. The aim was to reduce the quantity of a particular commodity to help the farmers obtain a parity price. . . .

In 1936, the United States Supreme Court declared the first AAA unconstitutional because it encroached into an area reserved for the states. . . .

Marketing agreements, still another part of the comprehensive program, were intended to regulate the flow of commodities on the market and trade practices as well. The object was to eliminate wild price fluctuations. Actual price-fixing through such arrangements was limited to one commodity: milk. . . .

The Soil Conservation and Domestic Allotment Act was passed within a period of two months. Passage of the new measure indicated that the farmers as well as the Administration were behind the AAA. . . .

Some interesting comparisons might be drawn between the first and second agricultural adjustment acts. The latter, instead of stressing crop controls, emphasized soil conservation.

The first act was based on the theory that agriculture was over-expanded and that a "straightforward drive" had to be made on production to reduce the output.

The second AAA, the Soil Conservation and Domestic Allotment Act, asserted that our land resources were being recklessly exploited and that it was necessary for the farmers to convert them into pasture, woodland, or legumes.

Soil conservation was stressed after the great drought of 1934 and the problems that grew out of soil and wind erosion. Payments were to be paid farmers cooperating to further soil conservation.

The accumulation of large stocks of food and other commodities convinced the Administration of the wisdom of storing some of the surplus of the "fat years" to provide for the nation during the "lean years."

A system of loans was devised to help accumulate these surpluses. This general scheme was the essence of the "ever-normal granary" plan. . . .

The aim was to maintain the prices of the surplus commodities by channeling them into the hands of those who needed them.

Similar but more restricted techniques were employed during the Federal Farm Board years. Surpluses were diverted into by-products, and where possible into the export market. . . .

In poor communities, food was furnished nursery schools and school lunch programs were fostered to provide food for the underprivileged and the undernourished.

In 1939 free food distribution was launched through normal trade channels. This marked the beginning of the food stamp plan. One on relief was given stamps by the proper agency which he could use to buy surplus foods that were on the accredited list of a cooperating retail merchant.

The merchant redeemed these stamps for cash through the Federal Surplus Commodities Corporation. By 1939, the food stamp plan was so successful that plans were made to extend it to other communities. . . .

Another phase of the New Deal farm program had to do with the extension of aid to farm families receiving low incomes. This was to be attempted by seeking to better the position of those on lands which needed improvements, or by transferring them from poor to better farm lands. Plans were devised to help these people become self-supporting.

Loans, seed, livestock and equipment were provided depending on the needs and qualifications of the individual involved. Those who were transferred from submarginal lands needed even greater aid.

Two significant agencies seeking to deal with farm tenancy were the Rural Resettlement Administration and the Farm Security Administration. The first was established in 1935; its purpose was to combat farm tenancy which was blamed for low farm incomes.

In 1936 a committee was appointed "to alleviate the shortcomings of our farm tenancy system." This resulted in the

Bankhead-Jones Tenancy Act. Loans were authorized to share-croppers, laborers and farm tenants to help them become landowners.

In 1937, the Farm Security Administration was organized as a successor of the Rural Resettlement Administration; it sought to carry out the provisions of the Bankhead-Jones Act and carry out projects launched by the Resettlement Administration.

The Rural Electrification Administration was another significant agency. Organized in 1935, the theory behind it was to furnish a larger portion of the rural population with electric current. The farmers were to be charged rates lower than those levied by the commercial agencies. . . .

On the credit side of the agricultural ledger, the New Dealers claimed that by 1939 some progress had been made toward agricultural recovery. Farm prices and incomes had risen. . . .

Progress had been made in teaching farmers the need of forest and soil conservation. Electric current was furnished those residing in remote areas, and headway was made in combating insects and diseases.

Credit facilities were expanded and some hope for a better future in farming was held out for marginal and submarginal producers. . . .

Reciprocal trade treaties seemed to offer an opportunity for recapturing some of the foreign markets the American producers previously enjoyed. . . .

Critics tended to emphasize the debit side of the agricultural ledger. A frequently heard argument was that the New Deal accomplished far less than it promised.

Farm incomes had risen but not to the levels the farmers would have liked.

FARM POLICY, 1940-52 [7]

For American agriculture the years 1940-1952 afforded a sharp contrast with the depression. Stimulated by the inflationary tendencies accompanying World War II, the ensuing cold war

[7] From "Parity and Surpluses," article by Colston Warne, professor of economics, Amherst College. *Current History.* 26:105-10. February 1954. Reprinted by permission.

and the Korean conflict, agriculture experienced thirteen years of generally increasing prices, high productivity, marked Government assistance, and substantial profits.

The nation, so long unsuccessful in coping with recurrent agricultural surpluses, moved into a war and defense decade in which the emphasis became fixed upon high farm output, accompanied by Government price assistance and crop planning. . . .

Prices of farm products during the thirteen-year period continued steadily upward until in 1948 they were 285 per cent of the level of 1910-1914. (They had been 95 per cent of that level in 1939.)

After a brief decline in 1949, farm prices rose in 1951 to a new crest of 302 per cent of 1910-1914. The index at the close of 1952 was 288. . . .

In other words, farm prices had in 1952 kept pace with increased farm costs, whereas in 1940 farm prices lagged 17 per cent behind the rise in costs.

Parity, which had been devised as a method of measuring the level of Government price support . . . became unfortunately a keystone in the wartime program of price ceilings and guaranteed prices. . . .

The mechanism of price parity which became thoroughly entrenched in the law during the 1940's unhappily interfered with war production and with price control and left many unsettled postwar problems.

It is understandable that farmers should seize upon "parity" as a slogan to sustain their incomes during depression, despite two obvious defects: First, no such device can accurately measure price equity for specific crops in a period of rapid mechanization both in industry and agriculture. Second, a price supported at parity levels tends to continue the unwise use of resources in fields in which demand is lagging, thus bringing Government accumulations of unsold surpluses. . . .

In legislation passed on October 2, 1942, ceiling prices were placed on farm commodities at parity levels or the highest price received by producers between January 1942 and September 15, 1942, whichever was higher. . . .

Much credit is due to Agriculture Secretary Claude Wickard for developing agricultural goals accenting human nutrition needs; accelerating the use of fertilizers; and seeking to allocate funds to make such goals attainable.

Yet the handicaps imposed by entrenched farm lobbies ultimately were able to force his resignation, and to waste badly needed resources upon the production of unessential crops. . . .

While it has been traditional for individualistic farm leaders to decry Government interference, it is most significant that Government price support of farm prices at near parity levels received strong approval by both the Republican and Democratic parties in the 1952 elections.

The Agricultural Act of 1949 had carried forward in amended form the basic parity principles of the Act of ten years before.

It designated six basic commodities for which price supports would be furnished through loans, purchases or other techniques. . . .

Other commodities might receive price support by action of the Secretary of Agriculture. The highest level of support is 90 per cent of parity; the lowest varies by commodities. . . .

This price support system was enacted by the farm bloc in Congress over the protests of Secretary of Agriculture Brannan, who felt that it did not get at the basic source of agricultural price problems. He sought instead a plan which would sustain the real income of the family farm, rather than maintaining prices by government purchase or loan techniques.

Succinctly, Brannan would allow prices for farm crops to find their own level in the market and at the same time directly subsidize cooperating eligible farmers to the extent that real agricultural income fell short of that in recent years.

Subsidy benefits would decline as operations became larger, thus favoring the "small" farmer. Production was to be held under control. . . .

Looked at in perspective, Government agricultural programs between 1945 and 1952 acted as an escalator which contributed to the inflationary trend; they occasioned unwieldy surpluses in many fields; and it was evident that drastic alterations would have to be made if stable agricultural prosperity and low consumer food prices were to be assured.

THE BRANNAN FARM PROGRAM [8]

The "Brannan Plan" [submitted by Secretary of Agriculture Charles F. Brannan in 1949 but never enacted by Congress] . . . recognizes the consumer interest in reasonable food prices to a much greater degree than most competing proposals. It tends to favor the two groups primarily concerned—dirt farmers and ordinary consumers—with a minimum of bonanzas and windfalls for the food processors, middlemen, and absentee owners of vast farm acreages who are frequently the ones who benefit most from "farm programs."

The plan as a whole, Consumers Union believes, warrants the support of consumers despite its shortcomings. Though it is intended primarily to benefit the farm population, the plan could help to stabilize our entire economy.

That some sort of farm plan is essential has . . . become a fixed principle of the American economic system. Secretary Brannan makes this point simply. "Price supports," he says, "are the farmer's equivalent of the laboring man's minimum-wage, social-security, and collective-bargaining arrangements."

The reasons why supports are needed stem from the fact that the farmer lives in an economy where the prices of most of the products he buys are set by monopolies, by open or tacit agreement among producers, or by simple restriction of production to hold prices up. The prices of the products he sells, on the other hand, are elastic. . . . The techniques which other segments of our economy use to stabilize prices are not open to the individual farmer acting alone. As a result, the cash income of ordinary farmers on ordinary farms has often, in the past, fallen below the level which would maintain a decent standard of living. Federal aid is needed to stabilize farm prices in conformity with those of the rest of the economy.

[8] From an article in *Consumer Reports*. 14:278-80. June 1949. Reprinted by permission.

This is peculiarly true because, inevitably, farmers acting by themselves will tend to turn even minor farm surpluses into catastrophic gluts. The cycle is simple. If supply exceeds demand, the price falls. The individual farmer finds his income cut while his taxes, mortgage interest, and other charges remain high. And he is no position, by himself, to adjust to this situation as many manufacturers do, by restricting production. Thus surpluses accumulate.

In classical economic theory, the corrective for this type of overproduction is the elimination of enough "producing units" to bring supply back into line with demand. In human terms, this means the bankruptcy of farm families, foreclosures on their mortgages, and untold human suffering. Certainly no American government in the foreseeable future will permit a recurrence of such conditions.

Furthermore, farm price supports are warranted by the need to keep the farm segment of our population in sufficiently prosperous condition to continue to consume the products of our cities. The rest of the country simply cannot remain prosperous while the farm population is depressed. And any substantial reduction in farm income would be almost certain to usher in a depression.

The most significant feature of the Brannan proposals, from the point of view of consumers, is the shift in emphasis from *commodity purchases* to *production payments* [i.e., direct Government payments to farmers covering the difference between the free market price and "a fair return" on non-storable commodities—Ed.]. The change should benefit consumers as well as farmers.

At present, the prices of potatoes, milk products, eggs, and some other commodities are being held up by Government purchases of these commodities in the open market. A less efficient means of stabilizing farm prices could hardly be imagined, short of having the Government make its purchases at corner grocery stores. It means, in effect, that everybody along the line takes a cut out of the Government handout before the residue, if any, reaches the farmer. Speculator, processor, warehouseman, middleman—each shares in the Government dollar supposedly spent to benefit the farmer.

The consumer is doubly penalized by the commodity purchase program. First, he pays the cost of the purchases in higher taxes. Second, he pays higher prices for his food as a result of the Government's running up of the price.

The commodity purchase program is self-defeating in another respect. When the price of potatoes, for example, is pegged at a relatively high level, two things happen. The high price causes consumers to buy fewer potatoes, while simultaneously it stimulates farmers to raise more. Thus commodity purchases may intensify the very supply-demand imbalance they were intended to remedy.

The *production payment* program is designed to avoid these difficulties. With respect to products subject to production payments, no attempt would be made to raise or maintain *food prices*. The price of potatoes, for example, might fall from the pegged level of $1.75 a bushel to $1 or even lower. However, if the *price received by the farmer* fell, on the average, below the support level, a production payment would be made directly to the farmer to raise the average farm price to the support level.

The immediate advantage to the consumer is readily apparent. Prices in retail stores would fall to their natural levels. As a result, consumption would tend to rise. The farmer, too, would benefit in a number of ways. He would get, directly and in full, the Federal payment, instead of getting indirectly what was left of Federal funds after speculators and middlemen had taken their profits. And he would benefit also from the larger market for his products stimulated by lower retail prices.

A second noteworthy feature of the Brannan proposals is the limitation on the size of the farms which will benefit from production payments. In theory, farm price support plans are justified by the need to maintain a decent standard of living for ordinary farm families. In practice, large corporations operating vast acreages on a semi-factory basis have received tens and even hundreds of thousands of dollars in "benefit payments" from farm appropriations. The Brannan proposals would limit the extent of participation in production payments. Each farm could participate to the extent of some 1800 "units" of production, a crop worth about $20,000 at present prices. (A "unit" is ten bushels of corn or the cash equivalent in other crops.) Farms producing more than this would get production payments only on the first 1800 units. Some 2 per cent of the farms, producing 25 per cent of the total dollar volume of farm products, would be affected by this limitation.

Some critics of the Brannan plan have argued that the participation limit is too high for channeling benefits to the "family farms" which most need them. On the other hand, the 1800-unit limitation is better than none.

Any price support plan tends to increase the production of those commodities which are already being heavily produced. If the price support system is not to be swamped by disastrous gluts, it must exact a ceiling on production as the condition for participation in benefit payments.

The Brannan proposals have been attacked as a "regimentation" of the farmer because of such provisions. . . . Brannan's answer is this:

> Farmers fought for the legal rights they now have to impose marketing limits upon themselves. In the view of those who did so, these rights represent an extension, not an infringement, of their freedom. I adhere to this principle.

The major type of control called for—marketing quotas—cannot be imposed unless approved by two thirds of the farmers concerned, voting in a referendum. Consumers, however, have no voice whatever in the determination of production control policy. A considerable improvement in the entire farm program, and one likely to win it added popular support, would be provision for consumer representation when basic policy determinations under the program are being made. . . .

The Brannan proposal would base [price] supports on the purchasing power of the farmer's dollar today, compared with its purchasing power over the ten-year test period. At present, Brannan calculates, the farmer needs $1.25 to purchase as much as he could get, on the average, for $1 during the decade 1939 to 1948. Accordingly, the support level for a crop today would be 25 per cent above its average price during the test decade.

There is room for argument whether this level is too high or too low. From one point of view, it would appear to continue the abnormally high price level of the war years [World War II] for a considerable period into the future. Brannan's reply is that the proposed farm price level would still leave farm purchasing power at a lower level than it has been for the past six years. The formula, in short, is a compromise.

A particularly interesting and urgent application of the "production payment" plan is suggested for milk. Brannan calls attention to the fact that while retail fresh milk prices have risen more or less steadily since 1947, consumption has been falling. He continues:

> We should be producing and consuming 150 million pounds of milk by now instead of something less than 120 million. If it is necessary to get milk down to the area of 15 cents a quart at retail in order to have maximum consumption, and use production payments to assure farmers a fair return, I think both farmers and consumers will want to do it. . . .

Much of the . . . criticism of the Brannan plan is actually applicable to any plan at all which aims at preventing catastrophic declines in farm prices. For example, it is charged that full operation of the plan would cost the taxpayers billions of dollars a year. This might be true, depending on the future trend of urban employment, prices generally, and other incalculables. On the other hand, given general prosperity, the plan might well exact little or no cost. Large sums are being spent . . . to hold up the price of such products as milk, butter, potatoes, and eggs in a wholly unreasonable manner. The same sums, rationally expended, could bring benefits to the farmer without pricing consumers out of the market.

A more significant criticism of the Brannan proposals is that they do not go nearly far enough. For example, Brannan makes a most convincing case for production payments as a means of supporting prices. But with respect to the staple farm crops— especially corn, wheat and cotton—he proposes to continue the older techniques of loans, purchase agreements, and spot purchases, all of which have had the effect of raising consumer prices unduly. Similarly, the limitation of benefit participation to the first 1800 units of a farm's production is not applicable to the major crops.

II. PRESENT FEDERAL FARM POLICY

EDITOR'S INTRODUCTION

This section recounts the efforts of the Eisenhower Administration to deal with the agricultural crisis. A glossary of terms used in farm-bill debates is given to orient the reader at the start.

In the second selection, Secretary of Agriculture Benson describes the problems "inherited" from previous administrations and tells what he has done to meet them. One of his predecessors, the author of the "Brannan Plan," takes issue with Secretary Benson's account of the situation he faced on taking office and with his efforts to cope with it.

Mr. Benson outlines in a speech the objectives of the present Administration as embodied in the President's special message to Congress in January 1956. The chairman of the Senate Committee on Agriculture next explains the Agricultural Act of 1956, as passed by Congress, which rejected much of the Administration's approach. The President tells in his veto message his reasons for rejecting the measure passed by the Congress. Finally, a newspaper correspondent analyzes the similarities and differences in the vetoed bill and the compromise measure ultimately enacted by Congress and signed by the President.

GLOSSARY OF FARM-BILL TERMS [1]

In the Senate debate on farm legislation the speeches are filled with terms that appear to be farm politics "gobbledygook." Here are some of the more important terms and their meanings:

SURPLUS. The amount of any farm commodity produced above what is set as a "normal supply." A "normal supply" is, generally speaking, the estimated domestic consumption, plus estimated exports, plus an allowance for carryover or cushion to guard against drought or other emergencies.

[1] From "Parity, Basic Crops, Soil Bank, etc.; Meanings of Terms in the Farm Bill," by William M. Blair, New York *Times* staff correspondent. New York *Times*. Section IV, p7. March 11, 1956. Reprinted by permission.

For example, if the "normal supply" of wheat is set for any given year at 100 million bushels, all production above that would be listed as surplus. Surpluses in such crops as wheat, corn, cotton and rice have helped create the present sag in the farm economy. Surpluses tend to depress market prices.

BASIC CROPS. These are six crops so designated by farm law. They are corn, cotton, wheat, rice, peanuts and tobacco. Price supports on these crops are mandatory. The legislative fight centers on these products.

NONBASICS. Six other products also so designated by farm law. They are dairy products, honey, tung nuts, wool and mohair.

OTHER CROPS. This designation also is applied by law. These crops are oats, barley, grain, sorghums, rye, dried beans, naval stores, cottonseed oil and soybeans. Price supports on these crops are permissive at the discretion of the Secretary of Agriculture.

PARITY. Parity prices are the dollars and cents prices that give to farm products the same buying or purchasing power they had in a selected base period when prices received by and prices paid by farmers were regarded as in good balance. This is spelled out in Federal law.

It has been put this way: If you can sell a truckload of corn and buy with the money received as much food, clothing, building materials, fertilizer, farm machinery and other living and production items as you could in a chosen favorable period in the past, then your corn is selling at a parity price.

RIGID PRICE SUPPORTS. These are supports maintained at 90 per cent of the parity price. Until last year [1955] rigid supports were mandatory on corn, wheat, cotton, rice, peanuts and tobacco. For example, if the computed parity price for corn was $1.80 a bushel, the Federal support price or guarantee to farmers was 90 per cent of that amount, or $1.62.

FLEXIBLE PRICE SUPPORTS. A range between 75 and 90 per cent of the parity price. This system is designed to discourage production through a lower support level in periods of overproduction . . . and encourage farm output in times of scarcity.

The Secretary of Agriculture follows law in determining the level under flexible supports. He sets the level by weighing various supply and demand factors. For example, he has set a national support rate of 81 per cent of parity, or $1.40 a bushel for the 1956 corn crop, compared with the 1955 level of 87 per cent, or $1.58 a bushel.

Rigid or mandatory 90 per cent supports on the designated basic crops except tobacco were dropped by a new act of Congress last year and replaced with the flexible supports. . . .

LOANS. These are bank loans guaranteed by the Government. They are designed to provide producers with a cash return for their products and strengthen market prices by withdrawing surplus output from markets.

To obtain a price support loan a farmer delivers to the Government part of his product. He gets cash at the support level that is then in effect. If, after a stated period, he finds he can get more for his product in the open market or finds another outlet for his commodity he can redeem the loan by paying back the money and 3.5 per cent interest.

If he finds that the market price is below the Government support after the stated period he gives the Government title to the product. As property of the Government the product is added to the Federal inventory.

CCC. The Commodity Credit Corporation, a Government agency that acts as the "banker" or operator of the Federal price support program. It is capitalized at $100 million subscribed by the United States. It has borrowing authority of $12.5 billion, of which nearly $8.5 billion is invested in price support operations at present.

SOIL BANK. This is the Administration's new triple-threat program aimed at (1) bolstering farm income with cash payments for cutting production, (2) helping to cut down surpluses already on hand and (3) getting inefficient and marginal farm land out of soil-depleting crops and into soil-building work.

The soil bank is in two parts:

ACREAGE RESERVE. A four-year "emergency" plan to obtain reduction of production in cotton, wheat, corn and rice. Payments are proposed to equal or exceed the net income a farmer would receive if his acres were planted and harvested. The payments may be in cash or kind. Production and grazing would be prohibited during the time the acres are in the reserve.

CONSERVATION RESERVE. The objective here is to transfer about 25 million acres of all kinds of crop land to forage, trees and water storage. The Government would share in establishing the acres in grasses and trees and pay farmers set amounts each year under contracts of not less than three years nor more than fifteen years.

BENSON'S PROGRAM, AS HE SEES IT [2]

Our critics will not succeed in their desperate attempt to mislead the American people into believing that farm prices and incomes are falling because of the flexible price supports put into operation by the Eisenhower Administration. The general level of all farm commodity prices has been skidding since 1951—and nearly three fifths of the decline in the farmer's economic position took place in the twenty-three months before this Administration came into office in January 1953, twenty-three months when supports were high and rigid. As provided in the Agricultural Act of 1954, flexible price supports on the basic commodities did not even start to come into effect until the 1955 crops were harvested—and then only on wheat, rice and corn.

There are three basic reasons why our farm families are in trouble. One is the imbalance between production and markets brought about by the war and the continuation of wartime price supports for ten years after the shooting stopped in Europe and Japan.

Another is record production of farm commodities in 1953-1955, despite acreage allotments and marketing quotas that have taken 29 million acres of wheat and cotton land out of cultivation in the past two years.

The third cause is the rigid cost structure and the high capital requirements of agriculture, plus a marketing system that

[2] From "Benson and Brannan Debate the Farm Issue"—Secretary of Agriculture Ezra Taft Benson's views. *Collier's*. 137:25-7+. April 13, 1956. Reprinted by permission.

now gives farmers only 38 cents out of the consumer food dollar.

These three basic causes have culminated in the mountainous surpluses that are our biggest farm headache today.

In December 1955, our Commodity Credit Corporation had an investment of $8.2 billion in price-supported commodities. Farm commodities owned outright by the Government totaled over $6.1 billion. Storage charges alone on this inventory of surpluses ran about $1 million a day.

We have made tremendous efforts to dispose of these stocks. During the past three years, we have moved out of storage and into use more than $4 billion worth of surplus commodities. Yet for each bushel equivalent of CCC stocks sold, about one and a half has replaced it in the stockpiles. . . .

If you were living on a farm or in a rural community thirty-five years ago, you probably remember the painful aftermath of World War I. The wartime markets for wheat, meat, corn and other crops collapsed. Within the space of one year, the general level of farm prices was cut almost in half. Farmers who were buying high-priced land lost their farms. Banks in rural communities closed right and left. Rural businesses were hard hit, too.

Congress did not want that to happen again. Therefore, early in World War II, Congress set rigid price supports at 90 per cent of parity on all crops important to the war effort. . . . The . . . measure . . . was to be in effect for as long as the war should last and for two full years after it was over.

In 1948 a Republican-led Congress and in 1949 a Democrat-led Congress—more than two full years after the war ended—passed legislation providing for an end to the rigid wartime supports and the gradual adoption of flexible, or variable, supports.

But before the new laws could take effect, certain self-styled friends of the farmer seized upon the issue as a political opportunity, claiming that we need rigid 90 per cent of parity supports to keep farm prices and income steady. Amendments were passed continuing high rigid supports on the basic commodities . . . through the 1954 crops.

When the Republican Administration took office in 1953, we were bound by law to support these crops at 90 per cent through 1954. And we have done so.

But President Eisenhower had pledged to study this entire question, and we have also done this.

One of our first acts . . . was to get under way the most comprehensive study of the entire support question ever made [covering more than sixty different survey groups]. . . .

The sentiment of these groups favored flexible rather than rigid supports. Upon this foundation the Agricultural Act of 1954 was built; it provided that price supports should gradually become flexible, beginning with the 1955 crops. . . .

On January 9 of this year President Eisenhower sent to the Congress a special message on agriculture. It contained the Administration's recommendations for building solidly on the sound, basic farm program enacted in 1954. . . .

The Agricultural Act of 1954 was not patchwork. It was, and remains, a sober, bipartisan attempt to work out a sound program. But no program can work effectively carrying on its back the massive surpluses this country has accumulated. . . .

The Eighty-third Republican Congress passed the Agricultural Trade Development and Assistance Act of 1954 to give us a more effective surplus-disposal tool, and we have used it, and other measures, with far more success than most people know.

Since July 1, 1953, . . . we have moved out of government storage and into use commodities that cost over $4 billion. Without these effective disposal operations, the CCC inventory of farm commodities would now be more than $10 billion, instead of $6.1 billion.

And we have disposed of these surpluses, not during a time of great world demand for agricultural commodities, but during a period when agricultural production in most countries was relatively high.

Last summer I appointed a full-time general sales manager to coordinate and push all CCC commodity disposal operations. (And I am appointing an agricultural surplus disposal administrator to speed up activities in this entire field.) We will emphasize sales for dollars, . . . but there will be no slackening of our efforts to move our surpluses into all available outlets, while making sure, as required by law, that Government surpluses will not be thrown on the market here at home and upset regular sales by agricultural producers and processors.

As for exports, we are pushing and we will continue to push an aggressive sales policy with all the vigor we can command, but we will not unduly disrupt world markets for other free nations. We will not "dump" our surpluses abroad. . . .

Farm problems cannot be resolved by one program method, such as price supports alone. We are following through on these other programs:

In the past two years farmers and ranchers have applied more soil conservation practices than in any previous two years in history.

We have developed a program for upstream protection of watersheds, to conserve soil and water and prevent floods.

We have given independence to the Farm Credit Administration and provided for farmer control of this agency—something farmers have wanted for years.

Under this Administration we have had the biggest expansion of grain storage facilities in all history. We have helped farmers take advantage of the storage-loan program.

The rural electrification program now provides more power to farm and rural families at lower costs than ever before. The rural telephone program is being expanded at a record rate.

We extended Social Security coverage to more than 5 million farm families and farm workers.

The school lunch program has been expanded and the special school milk program was started in which nearly 9 million children took part in 1954-1955. . . .

I would rather be right than Secretary of Agriculture. But I believe it is possible to be both.

AS BRANNAN SEES BENSON'S PROGRAM [3]

Besides abundance, we have prosperity—except for the farmers who have helped so much to create it. By the thou-

[3] From "Benson and Brannan Debate the Farm Issue"—former Secretary of Agriculture Charles F. Brannan's views. *Collier's.* 137:25-7+. April 13, 1956. Reprinted by permission.

sands, farmers are going broke and leaving the farms; last year
the national income soared to the highest point in our history,
while the farmer's income plunged more sharply than in any
year except 1921. A few months ago, the New York stock
market reached an all-time high, while the Iowa hog market fell
to a fifteen-year low. . . .

On October 1, 1952, at Columbia, South Carolina, General
Dwight D. Eisenhower had this to say about the farm program:
"I believe wholeheartedly and without any 'ifs' and 'buts' in
Federal programs to stabilize farm prices, including the present
program insuring 90 per cent of parity on all basic commodities."
Since then, the President's Administration has reneged on this
. . . promise to farmers and has reversed a Federal farm policy
based on twenty years of remarkably successful experience in the
Roosevelt and Truman Administrations.

The impact of this reversal upon our farmers is mirrored
in the chilly figures published by the President's Council of
Economic Advisers: Between 1952 and 1955, the annual net
farm income fell over 26 per cent . . . although the output
of farmers increased by 8 per cent. Department of Agriculture
reports show that during these same three years and as a result
of this decline in income, farmers' indebtedness almost
doubled. . . .

Yet, in the same period, corporate profits after taxes climbed
32 per cent, stockholders' incomes 10 per cent and stock prices
32 per cent.

Abandonment of the American farmer to the inexorable law
of supply and demand and the forces which manipulate the
market to their own ends account for this national economic
freak. These are the same forces that broke most of the farmers
in the late 1920's and broke the nation soon thereafter.

These forces were unleashed in 1953 by implementation of
the so-called "flexible" price support theory, to replace the full
parity support program which was the objective of the Democrats. The relative merit of these two conflicting methods has
been, and will continue to be, a raging political issue. . . .

Parity is the formula by which the relationship between
the selling price of farm crops and their cost of production in
a base period is reflected to a current date. . . .

An overly simplified definition might go like this: if a bushel of wheat sold for enough to buy a work shirt in 1939 (or whatever base period) it should sell for enough to buy a work shirt now. As the price of fertilizer, machinery, gasoline and other commodities farmers must buy goes up, the parity formula dictates that the price of the farm crops produced through use of these commodities shall go up. If costs go down, the parity price also goes down.

Hence, the parity formula is not "rigid." It is truly flexible in relation to costs of production.

Neither is parity high. By its very definition, parity means fair and equitable. One hundred per cent of parity is 100 per cent of fair. . . .

"High rigid" is a totally deceptive phrase. . . .

The confusion over price supports is compounded by the confusion over farm surpluses. The price support mechanism was not intended to and cannot control production.

Yet much of the confusion about price supports and surpluses was created by the Republican party's introduction of the "flexible price support" proposal. Its proponents start with the premise that surpluses of farm products have been created by the price support program they erroneously describe as "high, rigid." Thus, it follows, they contend, that Government supports must be withdrawn or reduced to whatever lower levels are necessary to discourage production.

They also maintain that lower prices to farmers will result in cheaper food for consumers, and because the amount which may be borrowed is reduced, Government costs will likewise go down. . . .

Briefly, here is how Federal price supports have worked up to now for the producers of storable crops such as cotton and corn:

If the farmer finds the price offered on the open market at harvest time less than the Government support level, as fixed by the parity formula, he may borrow 100 per cent of the Government's support price. . . .

Once this crop is under loan, the farmer has until the next harvest to redeem. This he will do if the market price goes up to the point where he can profit by paying back the borrowed money plus interest and storage charges. . . . If he doesn't redeem it before the next harvest, the farmer surrenders the collateral (his crop) to the Government and his note is canceled. . . .

The men who framed this farm program anticipated surpluses. And they furnished the Secretary of Agriculture with a device for releasing the Government from excessive costs whenever genuine surpluses of a price-supported crop develop.

Whenever the Secretary has felt that a surplus of a price-supported crop has accumulated, he has been authorized to schedule a referendum in which all growers of that commodity are invited to vote to decide whether they will accept production and marketing controls—in the form of acreage allotments and marketing quotas—with continued price support, or whether they will raise and market their crops free of any restrictions and without price supports.

In most cases, farmers have overwhelmingly elected to cut production and maintain the floor under prices. . . .

The decision of the present Administration to rely upon lowered prices to reduce production of supported crops and to make only halfhearted use of this production- and marketing-control authority accounts in major part for the current turmoil.

ADMINISTRATION'S FARM PROGRAM [4]

This is the Administration's farm program. It is my program, and it is your program because it came from the grass roots.

Here are the nine recommendations:

1. A soil bank to help get production and demand in balance and to promote the basic conservation job so vital to our national future.

2. An expanded surplus disposal program.

3. Strengthened programs for wheat, cotton, corn, rice, livestock, and other crops.

[4] From a talk by Secretary of Agriculture Ezra Taft Benson before National Council of Farmer Cooperative, Los Angeles, California, January 16, 1956. Department of Agriculture, Office of the Secretary, Washington 25, D.C. January 1956. p 1-12.

4. A dollar limit on price supports to any individual or farm.

5. An expanded rural development program.

6. A realistic and long-needed agricultural program for the Great Plains.

7. Sharply increased research, especially on new uses, markets, and improved marketing methods.

8. Ample credit for farm families, especially veterans just starting out.

9. Refunding of the Federal gasoline tax for gasoline used on the farm. . . .

While the soil bank [see Section V, Acreage "Retirement" Programs, below] will help adjust production and reduce surplus stocks coming in the back door, surplus disposal activities will help move CCC stocks out of the front door. . . .

We will seek new opportunities to barter unneeded surplus agricultural commodities for strategic materials. . . . We urge that CCC be permitted to sell surplus commodities into the domestic market at the support level plus carrying charges as at present. This would be helpful to farmers in reducing surpluses. . . .

We urge that sales of surplus agricultural commodities to other than friendly countries be permitted under conditions that protect our national interests.

Another recommendation is prompt enactment of the rural development program [see Section VI, Family and Low-Income Farms, below]. About 1.5 million farm families . . . have incomes of less than $1,000. . . . How much food and clothing, medical care, recreation and household equipment can a family buy in these days with such a small amount of money? In nearly one thousand counties more than half the families depend on the income they get from small, poorly paying farms. . . .

Another recommendation deals with the Great Plains program. This vast region, involving ten states which span the nation from Canada to Mexico, normally produces 60 per cent of our wheat and 35 per cent of our cattle. It contains 37 per cent of our land area, and 40 per cent of our cropland.

The Department of Agriculture has proposed a carefully considered "Program for the Great Plains," in which the land-use factor is made a primary consideration in programs which the Department operates. . . .

The goal to be achieved is a stable agriculture, a diversified source of income, and a progressively satisfactory livelihood over a sustained period for the people of the region. To achieve this goal, there must be a widespread use of good soil management and water conservation practices together with land use adjustments which will enable farmers and ranchers of the area to cope effectively with the climatic hazards they face.

Another recommendation calls for sharply expanded research to find new crops, new markets, new uses, to improve the efficiency of our agricultural marketing system, and to expand our backlog of fundamental scientific knowledge. . . .

How much will this program help agriculture now—this year of 1956? Will it mean better prices, more income, greater economic security? The answer is definitely yes. . . .

First let's take what would definitely be added income— the refunded tax for gasoline used on farms. About half the total of the gasoline tax paid by farmers would be refunded, and this is estimated at $60 million. . . .

Now let's take the acreage reserve. This represents assured income. Even though crops might fail, the cooperating farmer would still receive a certificate based on normal yields from the reserve acres. It would have a cash value. . . .

Further, the program calls for incentives high enough to make the program a success. This means, in simple language, a sure income from these acres equal to their normal net income, plus a little more, depending on the incentive level. The "plus" would be additional income in 1956.

But the biggest effect on farm prices and income should result from a new buoyancy in the market place. The surpluses we now hold have a smothering effect on market prices. . . . Our very best estimate indicates that farm prices right now might be as much as 10 per cent higher if we did not have these surpluses. Think of that!

We estimate that these surpluses reduced farm income by the staggering sum of more than $2 billion in 1955. Without these surpluses net farm income last year might have been as much as 20 per cent higher. . . .

What I have been saying about the acreage reserve applies also to the conservation reserve. Based on our recommendations, conservation payments in 1956 may total about $600 million. Of this, $250 million would be accounted for by the existing Agricultural Conservation Program and the remaining $350 million by the new conservation reserve.

The conservation reserve payments, while not a net addition to income, would help farmers establish grass, trees, and water on acres which today are in unneeded harvested crops. As in the case of the acreage reserve, the removal of these acres from harvested crops—and the provision that they should not be grazed for a number of years—should strengthen markets.

SENATE COMMITTEE'S BILL [5]

The Senate Committee on Agriculture and Forestry did not adopt a two-year extension of rigid 90 per cent of parity price supports for political reasons. On the contrary, the 8-7 vote which reinstated high price supports included three Republicans and five Democrats. The proportion of the membership voting against the proposal was similarly divided: four Republicans and three Democrats voted "Nay."

Why, then, did the Committee feel that rigid price supports should be reinstated?

The reason is a simple one, and at the same time a compelling one. Net farm income has dropped nearly $5 billion since 1951—from $14.8 billion to $10 billion in the third quarter of 1955. The farmer's share of the consumer's dollar spent for food products fell from 48 cents in 1951 to 39 cents in December of 1955. During approximately that same period, net corporate profits and total labor income increased by $3.5 billion and $46.5 billion respectively.

It was the considered judgment of the Committee that unless steps were taken to bolster falling farm income, the depressed

[5] From "Senator Allen J. Ellender [Democrat, Louisiana], Chairman of the Senate Committee on Agriculture and Forestry, Reports on the Committee's Program." Facts Forum. 3:3-7. April 1956. Reprinted by permission.

state of American agriculture would spread into and infect other segments of our economy.

We considered a number of ways to increase farm income, and increase it substantially and immediately. We found that as to the basic commodities only one—an immediate increase in price support levels—would achieve the desired end, short of outright subsidy payments which neither the farmer nor the Congress desired. In the hope of bolstering farm prices of non-basics, including livestock, we have recommended an appropriation of $250 million to supplement Section 32 funds (used to purchase surplus perishable commodities for the school lunch and similar programs).

The question has frequently been raised, "Why did not the Committee confine its bill to recommendations in the President's farm message?"

The soil bank, the Great Plains program, the rural redevelopment program—all suggested to the Congress by President Eisenhower—will bring some good over a long-term period. By permitting acres to remain idle, they will doubtless result in reducing our carry-over in most crops now in surplus, and thereby cause market prices to rise, if enough time elapses. But our farmers cannot wait two years or five years for relief; they need help now, and immediate assistance is what the Committee on Agriculture and Forestry voted to extend to them.

It should be noted that the immediate increase in price support levels does not stand alone in the suggested farm program; included also were the long-range programs recommended by the President—and they were included for good reason.

It should also be noted that the inclusion of mandatory 90 per cent of parity price supports for five of the six basic commodities is limited to a two-year period. It is our hope that at the expiration of this period, the decline in farm income will have been effectively halted, that the long-range programs outlined by the President and included in the Committee's bill will have taken hold and that our farmers will not be in the dire straits they are today. . . .

One objection frequently raised was that 90 per cent of parity would nullify the soil bank.

This is poppycock. The Secretary of Agriculture would remain empowered to control acreages planted to supported commodities and to impose marketing quotas. As a matter of fact, all production of the six basic commodities in 1956 will be so controlled. Violators are subjected to heavy penalties, with the single exception of the farmers who grow corn. The corn program is on a quasi-voluntary basis as far as participation and compliance are concerned.

The fact to be remembered is that, whether price supports are flexible or fixed, whether they are at 75 per cent of parity, or 90 per cent of parity, acreage allotments and marketing quotas of the same magnitude are involved. The only thing the Committee bill seeks to do is increase the income a farmer can expect from these acreages; it would not increase acreage allotments, nor would it unduly stimulate production on the acreage already allocated to farmers who have voted in local referendums to participate in the Government price support program and to accept acreage controls. The same amounts of acreage will be allotted to the basic crops and will be planted to these crops in 1956, either with or without the 90 per cent parity support feature of the Committee bill. Nor will 90 per cent parity supports bring about increased yields per acre in 1956. On the contrary, the history of our farm program has shown that during periods of depressed returns, farmers try harder to increase their production in order to compensate for the lower per-unit market value of their crops.

As to the specific mathematics of the charge that high price supports will nullify the soil bank, let us take a concrete example.

Farmer A owns a 500-acre wheat farm. His acreage allotment for wheat during the 1956 crop year is, say, 100 acres. Under the flexible price support program his production on this 100 acres would be supported at about 76 per cent of parity. Under the Senate Agriculture Committee's bill this production would be supported at 90 per cent of parity. There would be no increase in the amount of acreage that Farmer A could plant. The only increase would be the immediate 14 per cent increase in the amount of income Farmer A would realize from production grown on his acreage allotment.

A part of the remaining 400 acres of Farmer A's land could be placed in the conservation reserve program of the soil bank; that is, Farmer A could agree to put his land into grass or trees and contract not to graze it, and he would receive annual Government payments for so doing.

As a matter of fact, it would seem to me that under the program of high price supports voted by the Committee, a farmer would have additional incentive to place some of his cultivable land in the soil bank than he would otherwise. In the first place, he would receive more income than under the sliding scale program; he would therefore feel less need for planting his remaining acres to feed grains or some secondary crop in order to supplement his income and would therefore be inclined to participate in the conservation reserve plan.

I believe, too, that with 90 per cent of parity price supports farmers would have more incentive not to plant their full acreage allotment, but instead to place some of their allotted acres into the acreage reserve program of the soil bank. Here is why:

Payments to stimulate participation in the acreage reserve will undoubtedly be based on a fixed percentage of the parity value of the existing support level. It would follow, then, that a higher support level would bring a higher incentive payment and, with it, a higher participation in the acreage reserve and a consequent lowering of the amount of acreage actually planted to the basic crops. Conversely, it would seem that lower farm prices would actually imperil the President's soil bank program rather than assist it.

We have also been criticized for not making participation in the so-called "acreage reserve" mandatory, instead of leaving it on a voluntary basis.

This participation was made voluntary for good reason. Our farm producers had already voted on the issue of whether they wanted acreage allotments. Their vote had been favorable, and it was predicated on participating farmers' planting all of the acreage allotted to them. Our Committee felt it would be morally as well as probably legally wrong for the Congress to impose a further condition on the planting of these acres—one which had not been voted on by the farmers at the time of the crop referendums, and one which would reduce their allotted acreage by a substantial amount—perhaps as much as 20 per cent.

However, the overriding objective of the Committee was to bolster farm income immediately. We felt, and I believe justifiably, that if the present price decline were permitted to continue for any appreciable time, many hundreds more of small farmers would be squeezed out of business; the trend toward "bigness" in agriculture, with its accompanying quasi-monopolistic characteristics and attendant dangers, would be accelerated. Even more dangerous, we felt that a depressed agriculture, bringing with it lowered farm purchasing power, would soon affect the entire economic structure of our nation.

PRESIDENT'S VETO MESSAGE [6]

I am returning herewith, without my approval, H.R. 12, designated as the "Agricultural Act of 1956." . . .

Our farm families are suffering reduced incomes. They had a right to expect workable and beneficial legislation to help solve their problems. This bill does not meet their needs. . . .

The problem is price-depressing surpluses. Excess stocks of certain farm commodities have mounted to market-destroying, price-depressing size as a result of wartime price incentives too long continued. Any forward-looking, sound program to meet the needs of farm people must remove the burden of these accumulations. They are depressing net farm income by many hundreds of millions of dollars a year.

H.R. 12 would not correct this situation. It would encourage more surpluses. It would do harm to every agricultural region of the country and also to the interests of consumers. Thus it fails to meet the test of being good for farmers and fair to all our people.

[6] From "Agricultural Act of 1956; Message from the President of the United States Returning Without Approval the bill (H.R. 12) Designated as the 'Agricultural Act of 1956.' " (House Document no380) 84th Congress, 2d session. Superintendent of Documents. Washington 25, D.C. April 16, 1956. p 1-5.

The bill is self-defeating. The soil bank proposal has been incorporated. This would be constructive, had it not been encumbered by contradictory provisions. The soil bank would provide an income incentive to farmers to reduce production temporarily so that surplus stocks might be reduced. Other provisions of this bill, however, would result in an equal or greater incentive to increase production and accumulate more surplus.

Among the provisions which make this bill unacceptable are: (1) The return to a wartime rigid 90 per cent of parity supports for the basic commodities; (2) Dual parity for wheat, corn, cotton and peanuts; (3) Mandatory price supports for feed grains; (4) Multiple price plans for wheat and rice. The effect of these provisions would be to increase the amount of Government control and further add to our price-depressing surpluses.

Specific objections relative to each of these provisions may be summarized as follows:

Price supports at wartime 90 per cent of parity on basic crops were in effect in each year from 1944 through 1954. They were not responsible for the high commodity prices and high farm income of wartime and the immediate postwar years. Prices were then above support levels due to wartime inflation and the insatiable markets associated with war. Neither did 90 per cent supports prevent prices from falling as postwar surplus stocks began to accumulate.

Price supports at wartime 90 per cent on the six designated basic crops did encourage production of these crops relative to others. At the same time consumption was discouraged and the use of substitutes was stimulated. Market outlets shrank, and surplus accumulations mounted. Acreage controls had to be invoked, thereby rationing the right to produce. Wheat acreage was reduced from 79 to an allotment of 62 and then to the present 55 million acres. Cotton was cut from 25 to 20 and then on down to the present 17 million acres. These drastic reductions, forced by the application of the price support law, penalized many farmers directly by resulting in shrunken volume and uneconomic farming operations. In addition, acreage diverted from the basic crops shifted surplus problems into many other crops and livestock. Now almost every farmer is adversely affected, regardless of what crops or livestock he raises.

If wartime rigid 90 per cent supports were the answer to the problem of our farm families, there would now be no problem.

Farm incomes have declined in every year except one between 1947 and 1954, and in all these years 90 per cent supports were in effect.

Farmers are not interested in price alone. What they really want for their families is more net income, which is affected by volume and costs as well as by price. The 90 per cent of parity approach focuses on support price alone.

To return now to wartime 90 per cent supports would be wrong. Production would be stimulated. Markets would be further destroyed, instead of expanded, as must be done. More surplus would accumulate—and surpluses are price depressing. Regimentation by ever stricter production controls would be the end result. It is inconceivable that we should ask farm families to go deeper into this self-defeating round of cause and effect.

The provision for dual parity would result in a permanent double standard of parity for determining price supports. Four crops would receive preferential treatment out of 160 products for which parity prices are figured. There is no justification in logic or in equity for such preferential treatment.

Particularly is this true because, under the working of the modernized parity formula enacted by the Congress, increasing the parity prices of some commodities automatically lowers the parity prices of all other commodities. If parity prices for wheat, corn, cotton and peanuts are to be higher, then parity prices of the other products must be lower.

To whatever degree prices would be further artificially raised there would be a corresponding stimulus to production, more controls on farmers, reduced consumption, increased accumulations, and lower prices in the market.

Such a device for parity manipulations could destroy the parity concept itself. It places a potent weapon in the hands of opponents of all price supports for farmers. We have no right to place the welfare of our farm families in such jeopardy.

The provision for mandatory supports on the feed grains would create more problems for farmers. The market for feed grains would shrink as livestock production would come to depend more on forage and less on grain. The flow of feed grains into Government stocks would increase and production controls would necessarily be intensified. Price relationships between feed, livestock and livestock products would be distorted. Producers of feeder cattle, feeder lambs and feeder pigs would be faced with downward pressure on prices. An imbalance would develop between feed crops and livestock products, with all its adverse consequences.

The multiple-price plans for wheat and rice would have adverse effects upon producers of other crops, upon our relations with friendly foreign nations, and upon our consumers.

There are other serious defects in the bill, such as certain provisions found in the section dealing with the dairy industry. Still other features are administratively bad and would require the hiring of thousands of additional inspectors and enforcers.

I recognize that the restoration by H.R. 12 of wartime mandatory 90 per cent price supports applies only to 1956 crops. This, in combination with other objectionable features of the bill, would put us back on the old road which has proved so harmful to farmers.

Bad as some provisions of this bill are, I would have signed it if in total it could be interpreted as sound and good for farmers and the nation.

After the most careful analysis I conclude that the bill is contradictory and self-defeating even as an emergency relief measure and it would lead to such serious consequences in additional surpluses and production controls as to further threaten the income and the welfare of our farm people.

Because the good features of the bill are combined with so much that would be detrimental to farmers' welfare, to sign it would be to retreat rather than advance toward a brighter future for our farm families.

We now have sound and forward-looking legislation in the Agricultural Act of 1954. Neither that act, nor any other, can become fully effective so long as it is smothered under the vast surpluses that have accumulated. We imperatively need remedial legislation to remove this burden and enable the fundamentally sound program provided in the Act of 1954 to become workable. Such remedial measures were proposed in my message of January 9.

I am keenly mindful that the failure of the Congress to enact a good new farm bill can have unfavorable effects on farm income in 1956, unless prompt administrative efforts to offset them are made immediately. Particularly, the failure to enact a soil bank before planting time this year makes such administrative efforts imperative.

Consequently, we are going to take prompt and decisive administrative action to improve farm income now. I have conferred with the Secretary of Agriculture, and the Administration is moving immediately on four major fronts:

In 1956 price supports on five of the basic crops—wheat, corn, cotton, rice and peanuts—will be set at a level of at least 82.5 per cent of parity. Tobacco will be supported as voted in the referendum in accordance with existing law.

Within this range of price support flexibility the Administration intends to set minimum support levels that will result in a national average of:

Wheat at $2 a bushel.

Corn at $1.50 a bushel.

Rice at $4.50 per hundred pounds.

A separate support for corn not under acreage control in the commercial corn area will be announced at an early date.

Price supports on cotton and peanuts have not yet been announced, but will be at least 82.5 per cent of parity.

The Secretary of Agriculture will announce shortly the details of the new cotton export sales program.

For this year the support price of manufacturing milk will be increased to $3.25 per hundred pounds. The support price of butterfat will be increased to 58.6 cents a pound.

We will use Department of Agriculture funds, where assistance will be constructive, to strengthen the prices of perishable farm commodities. We will have well over $400 million for that purpose for the year beginning July 1.

These actions, the Administration will take immediately.

I now request Congress to pass a straight soil bank bill as promptly as possible. It should be in operation before fall seeding for next year's crops. It is vital that we get the soil bank authorized in this session of the Congress. There is general agreement on it. I am ready to sign a sound soil bank act as soon as Congress sends it to me. That can be accomplished in a very few days if the leadership in Congress will undertake the task.

This combined program of administrative action and legislative enactment will begin now to improve the income and welfare of all our farm families.

Here is a challenge for both the legislative and executive branches of the Federal Government.

ORIGINAL AND REVISED BILLS COMPARED [7]

The House of Representatives approved a compromise farm bill . . . [May 23, 1956] 304 to 59, and sent it to the White House.

President Eisenhower . . . vetoed a broader measure April 16. [He signed the new bill May 29—Ed.] Provisions to which he objected either have been omitted or watered down to the Administration's apparent satisfaction.

The new measure . . . is especially tailored to please large numbers of midwestern farmers, whose votes next November could be decisive for either party. . . .

Aside from the soil bank, the most expensive features of the vetoed bill in terms of consumer prices have been stripped from the new measure or sharply modified.

President Eisenhower, in his veto message, specifically objected to four of them. On those four points, the two bills differ as follows:

[7] From "Revised Farm Bill Sent to President," by John D. Morris, New York *Times* Washington correspondent. New York *Times*. p 1+. May 24, 1956. Reprinted by permission.

Vetoed Bill—The Administration's flexible price support program would have been scrapped by requiring the Government to support prices of wheat, cotton, corn, rice and peanuts—classified as "basic commodities"—at 90 per cent of parity in 1956. Parity is a variable price designed to give farmers a fair return in terms of purchasing power.

New Bill—No comparable provision. Authority to fix support levels at 75 to 90 per cent of parity is retained.

Vetoed Bill—Mandatory support levels for rye, oats, barley and grain sorghums would have been tied to the support price of corn, and acreage reductions would have been required. This would have meant an immediate increase to 85 per cent of parity for feed grains, which are now supported at 70 per cent.

New Bill—Feed grain prices must be supported at 76 per cent of parity in 1956. This was a "compromise" devised by the Administration.

Vetoed Bill—The Administration would have been required to calculate parity for basic commodities on whichever of two formulas produced the higher price. This would have meant an increase in support levels.

New Bill—A "transitional" parity price, now in effect, must be maintained through 1957 for corn, wheat and peanuts. A 5 per cent reduction was scheduled under existing law.

Vetoed Bill—The Administration would have been directed to dispose of surplus rice abroad at prices below the domestic support level. A similar system for wheat would have been contingent upon a referendum of wheat farmers.

New Bill—A two-price system for rice is made discretionary with the Secretary of Agriculture. There is no such provision for wheat. . . .

Following are other major differences between the two measures:

Vetoed Bill—Mandatory supports for dairy products would have been fixed to 80 to 90 per cent of parity. They are now 75 to 90 per cent.

New Bill—No comparable provision.

Vetoed Bill—Acreage allotments on cotton would have been frozen at present levels for 1957 and 1958. A floor on rice acreage allotments in 1956 would have been set at 85 per cent of the 1955 total.

New Bill—National allotments on cotton and rice are frozen through 1958 at present levels. Cotton allotments may be reduced in any state, but no more than 1 per cent a year.

The new bill contains one major provision omitted from the vetoed measure. It requires the Administration, despite State Department objections, to dispose of surplus cotton stocks in foreign markets at or below competitive world prices.

Following are other provisions that also were contained in the vetoed bill:

A $500 million increase in funds for Government purchase of pork and other perishables in surplus supply. About $300 million a year is already available.

An authorization of $200 million for payment of ocean freight on surpluses disposed of through welfare organizations. This is in addition to $300 million previously available.

Studies by the Secretary of Agriculture covering new methods of disposing of surplus stocks, the price relationships of forest products and other subjects.

Establishment of the Office of Surplus Disposal Administrator to speed disposal programs.

Creation of a commission to study industrial uses of farm products to help reduce surpluses.

The two measures also gave authority to the Secretary of Agriculture to process and package surplus commodities for home use and donate surplus food to penal institutions.

III. PARITY AND PRICE SUPPORTS

EDITOR'S INTRODUCTION

This section is the first of four dealing with specific phases of the farm-policy debate. Of these none has been more widely or more vehemently argued than the merits of price supports and at what levels they should be offered.

The section opens with an exposition of support programs currently in operation by a specialist of the Commodity Stabilization Service of the United States Department of Agriculture.

The argument for high and rigid supports is presented by a state Farmers Union official in a statement to the Senate Committee on Agriculture and in a pamphlet of the National Farmers Union. The counter-arguments are offered in selections by a food research specialist and the Committee for Economic Development, a research group composed principally of representatives of business, finance, and industry.

A specialist of the Agricultural Marketing Service tells, in the final article of this section, just how the consumer's food dollar is shared by the farmer with food processors and distributors.

CURRENT PRICE SUPPORT ACTIVITIES [1]

The United States Department of Agriculture carries on a number of operations aimed at protecting prices received by farmers for agricultural commodities. These operations, commonly referred to as "price programs," include the price support, International Wheat Agreement . . . special school milk, marketing agreement and order, and sugar programs. . . .

Under the price support program, price minimums or "floors" are established for a number of commodities. Support is

[1] From *Price Programs*, by Harry S. Henderson, Information Division, Commodity Stabilization Service, and others. (Agricultural Information Bulletin no135) Department of Agriculture. Washington 25, D.C. 1953. p 1, 2, 43-6, 63-4.

achieved through loans, purchases, purchase agreements, and, in the case of wool and mohair, through payments. . . .

The International Wheat Agreement seeks to assure markets for wheat to exporting countries and supplies of wheat to importing countries at equitable prices. Under the Agreement, the United States is obligated to sell specified quantities of wheat to importing countries if the importing countries offer the maximum Agreement price; and the importing countries are obligated to buy specified quantities of wheat from the United States if the United States offers the wheat for sale at the minimum Agreement price.

Removal of surpluses, with consequent strengthening of prices, is the objective. . . . Legislation makes an amount equal to 30 per cent of the receipts collected under the customs laws available for encouraging the exportation of agricultural commodities and products; encouraging the domestic consumption of commodities and products by diverting them from the normal channels of trade or by increasing their use among persons in low-income groups; and reestablishing farmers' purchasing power by making payments in connection with the normal production of any agricultural commodity for domestic consumption.

The special school milk program encourages increased consumption of milk, thereby strengthening milk prices as well as improving diets of school children.

Marketing agreement and order programs enable farmers to establish and maintain orderly marketing conditions for certain agricultural commodities and their products. Milk-order programs establish equitable minimum prices that handlers or distributors are required to pay producers for milk going into various uses. For commodities other than milk—principally tree fruits, tree nuts, and vegetables—minimum prices are not established; but prices are strengthened through control of quantity, quality, and rate of shipment from producing areas.

The sugar program stabilizes prices through the regulation of imports of sugar from foreign areas and marketings of sugar produced in domestic areas. . . .

Price support operations carried on by the United States Department of Agriculture through the Commodity Credit Corporation seek to establish price minimums or "floors" for a number of agricultural commodities. . . .

Support for corn, cotton, wheat, rice, tobacco and peanuts—the basic commodities, is mandatory.

Support also is mandatory for certain designated nonbasic commodities—wool, mohair, tung nuts, honey, milk, and butterfat.

Support for other commodities is permissive; that is, discretionary with the Secretary of Agriculture.

One farmer has defined the parity price this way: "If you can sell a truckload of wheat and buy with the money as much food, clothing, building materials, farm machinery, fertilizer, and the like as you could in the five years 1910-1914, your wheat is selling at the parity price." That farmer has a good understanding of the parity principle and his definition, as far as it goes, is accurate.

Parity prices are the dollars-and-cents prices that give to farm commodities the same buying or purchasing power the commodities had in a selected base period when prices received and paid by farmers were considered to be in good balance. This purchasing power is measured in terms of (1) prices of commodities and services that farmers buy, (2) interest on farm indebtedness secured by farm real estate, (3) taxes on farm real estate, and (4), except for commodities still on the "old" or "transitional" parity bases, cash wage rates paid to hired farm labor. Parity prices are calculated in terms of prices received by farmers in the local markets in which they ordinarily sell. Therefore, parity prices apply to the average of all classes and grades of the commodity as sold by all farmers in the United States, except in the case of a few commodities. For fruits and vegetables, those sold for fresh use and those sold for processing are usually considered as separate commodities, and parity prices for fresh and processing categories are calculated for many of these crops.

Where necessary in connection with a particular program, average or normal differentials for different varieties, classes, or grades of a commodity and average or normal spreads between different markets, methods of sale, or locations are calculated and applied to the national average support level or to the parity price. Differentials may also be established for seasonal differences, especially where there is a reasonably regular and well-defined seasonal movement. Such spreads or differentials, of course, need adjusting or recalculating from time to time because of changes in methods of processing, in marketing and transportation costs, and in the distribution of supplies relative to demand.

Parity prices are computed in accordance with provisions of the Agricultural Adjustment Act of 1938, as amended by the Agricultural Acts of 1948, 1949, and 1954. Under this legislation a modernized or "new" parity formula is provided. . . . The modernized parity formula not only retains the 1910-14 base as the standard for equality between prices received for farm products on the one hand and prices paid by farmers for goods and services on the other, but it also establishes relationships among parity prices of farm products that reflect average price relationships during the immediately preceding ten-year period.

To prevent a sharp drop in the parity prices for basic commodities when computations are shifted from the "old" to the "new" formula, the legislation provides that through 1955 the parity prices for basic commodities shall not be less than the parity price computed by the procedure used prior to January 1, 1950. In order to cushion any reductions thereafter, the law provides that the parity price for basic commodities shall not be less than 95 per cent of the "old formula" parity during 1956, 90 per cent during 1957, 85 per cent during 1958, and so on until all these basic commodities have shifted to the new formula.

A similar cushioning effect for nonbasic commodities prevents the parity price from being less than the "transitional" parity price. The transitional parity price in 1955 is 70 per cent of prices as computed by the "old" formula and will decrease at 5 per cent per year until prices of all commodities have completed their transition to the "new" formula.

To summarize, the "effective parity price" is as follows:

For basic commodities:

(Through 1955): The higher of (1) the parity price computed by the "old" formula or (2) the parity price computed by the "new" formula.

(After 1955): The higher of (1) the parity price computed by the "new" formula or (2) the "transitional" parity price.

For nonbasic commodities:

(In 1955 and subsequent years): The "transitional" parity price, until such time as the parity price computed by the "new" formula is higher than the "transitional" parity price.

The Commodity Credit Corporation the [Government agency responsible for maintaining price supports] was organized October 17, 1933. . . . Originally incorporated under the laws of the State of Delaware, CCC was managed and operated in close affiliation with the Reconstruction Finance Corporation up to July 1, 1939, as an agency of the United States. On that date, CCC was transferred to and made a part of the United States Department of Agriculture.

Approval of the Commodity Credit Corporation Charter Act . . . on June 29, 1948, established CCC . . . as an agency of the United States under a permanent Federal charter. . . . Congress . . . [on] June 7, 1949, amended the Charter Act in several important respects.

The Charter Act, as amended, authorizes CCC to: (1) Support prices of agricultural commodities through loans, purchases, payments, and other operations; (2) make available materials and facilities required in the production and marketing of agricultural commodities; (3) procure agricultural commodities for sale to other Government agencies, foreign governments, and domestic, foreign, or international relief or rehabilitation agencies, and to meet domestic requirements; (4) remove and dispose of surplus agricultural commodities; (5) increase domestic consumption of agricultural commodities through development of new markets, marketing facilities, and uses; (6) export or cause to be exported, or aid in the development of foreign markets for, agricultural commodities; and (7) carry out such other operations as Congress may specifically authorize or provide for.

CCC is directed to utilize to the maximum extent practicable, the customary channels, facilities, and arrangements of trade and commerce in carrying on purchasing and selling operations (except sales to other Government agencies), and in conducting warehousing, transporting, processing, and handling operations.

CCC may contract for the use of plants and facilities for the handling, storing, processing, servicing, and transporting of agricultural commodities subject to its control. CCC has authority to acquire personal property and to rent or lease office space necessary for the conduct of its business. It is prohibited from acquiring real property or any interest therein except for the purposes of protecting its financial interests and for providing adequate storage to carry out its programs effectively and efficiently. No refrigerated cold-storage facilities may be constructed or purchased except with funds specifically provided by Congress for that purpose.

To encourage storage of grain on farms, CCC is directed to make loans available to grain producers for financing the construction or purchase of suitable storage.

CCC is authorized to accept strategic and critical materials produced abroad in exchange for agricultural commodities acquired by it. Strategic and critical materials so acquired shall, to the extent approved by the Director of the Office of Defense Mobilization, be transferred to the stockpile, and, when transferred, CCC shall be reimbursed in an amount equal to the fair market value of the material transferred. CCC also is authorized to acquire, hold, or dispose of strategic materials as it deems advisable in carrying out its functions and protecting its assets.

Borrowings by CCC (other than trust deposits and advances received on sales) and obligations to purchase loans held by lending agencies must not exceed $10 billion at any one time. CCC is capitalized at $100 million, subscribed by the United States. Interest must be paid to the United States Treasury on the capital stock—and on the amount of the obligations of CCC purchased by the Secretary of the Treasury—at such rates as may be determined by the Secretary of the Treasury.

Management of CCC is vested in a board of directors, subject to the general supervision and direction of the Secretary of Agriculture, who is an ex-officio director and is chairman of the board. The board consists of six members (in addition to the Secretary of Agriculture), who are appointed by the President of the United States by and with the advice and consent of the Senate.

The Commodity Credit Corporation Charter Act, as amended, provides for an advisory board consisting of five members appointed by the President of the United States. Not more than three of the members shall belong to the same political party. The advisory board is required to meet at the call of the Secretary of Agriculture at least every ninety days. The function of this board, which is made up of members having broad agricultural and business experience, is to survey the general policies of CCC, including those connected with lending and price support programs.

To carry on its operations, CCC makes broad use of the personnel and facilities of the Commodity Stabilization Service.

FOR HIGH, RIGID SUPPORTS [2]

At a recent policy-development meeting of my county farm bureau, with an attendance of a conservative two hundred members in attendance, 95 per cent went on record as favoring 100 per cent of parity price supports supplemented by reasonable restrictions on production. These objectives are very divergent from those expressed by top officials of Illinois Agricultural Association and American Farm Bureau Federation. Objectives and recommendations of the National Farmers Union dominated the thinking of farm bureau membership.

I disagree with Secretary of Agriculture Benson in his view that what he refers to as high rigid price supports are responsible for farm surpluses. Farmers are production minded. At best, a higher support price on one crop would only be responsible for a decision to seed a plot in a higher supported crop rather than a lower supported one. Most crops concerned have acreage allotments anyway. In the next place, how can 90 per cent supports be termed high when they are still 10 per cent below what the Government concedes to be fair and equitable? Again, how can they be rigid if geared to parity which is supposed to fluctuate? . . . .

    [2] From statement filed by Ralph S. Bradley, president, Illinois Farmers Union, with Senate Committee on Agriculture and Forestry at hearings on proposed modification of the general farm plan, Des Moines, Iowa, October 26, 1955. In *Price Support Program*; hearings, October 23, 1955-January 23, 1956. 84th Congress, 2d session. Superintendent of Documents, Washington 25, D.C. 1956. p882-4.

The consumer need not pay one cent more for his food to return a full 100 per cent of parity to the farm level. I refer you to the profit and loss statement of Kraft, a division of National Dairies. Their latest report showed a 31 per cent increase in net profits, while the dairy industry took it on the nose for a 26 per cent loss. This points up that this 26 per cent that the farmer did not get was not lost but it just stayed in the hands of the processor. It seems only fair that Kraft could have been satisfied with a normal increase in profits, and, therefore, returned to the farm its fair share.

I do not single out Kraft as the only one whose profit and loss statements show this situation, but offer it as one of several.

Since this situation is being keenly felt by farmers, they, quite naturally, are seeking out the leadership of someone who has a bold, forthright agricultural program that can be spelled out to give them faith to cling to. It must be remembered that in 1952 the farm issue was not a partisan political issue among the farmers themselves, since both candidates indicated to the farmers that they were truly interested in agriculture and, therefore, promised a good, sound, legislative agricultural program. And since both Mr. Stevenson and Mr. Eisenhower had assured the farmers that they were interested in them getting their full parity for the food and fiber they produced, the farm issue was no longer a contingent factor.

However, it is history now that Mr. Eisenhower broke faith with that promise, and it is through the windows of broken faith that the farmers are looking today, and quite naturally will be skeptical to the promises of any candidate who aspires to the great office of the presidency of the United States. And since the farm families are in such real trouble that they cannot afford to buy any vague promises such as "I am for 100 per cent of parity," or "Farmers are entitled to a full share of the economy" kind of thing, they will be looking for someone with a bold approach to this agriculture situation. It is not enough to say that one is in favor of the farmers making money, but rather the farmers will be waiting and watching for bold leadership who dares take his stand and spells out in detail a farm program that will place responsibility upon farmers, Government, and consumers.

I am sure the farmer is realistic enough to accept his responsibility in bringing into proper harmony the law of supply and demand within a reasonable focus. However, he will demand devices of Government to give him necessary protection against manipulated dishonesty in the marketing of his products.

Agriculture needs a bold leadership who has a philosophical concept of agriculture that is based upon the preservation of the family-farm type of agriculture.

WHY THE FARMER NEEDS FULL PARITY [3]

"Farm production is a two-way road," says the Department of Agriculture. "Down one road the farmer sends dollars, supplies, manpower, and provides raw materials for the towns and cities. Down the other road the towns and cities send the farmer dollars for his products, manpower and machines, chemicals, energy, scientific knowledge, and other goods and services essential to present-day high level farm production."

Once upon a time, not more than forty years ago, this two-way street was more or less a one-way lane. Farmers produced most of their own power, raised most of their own fuel, and bought little or no commercial fertilizer. They were as independent of the city and the goods it produced as they possibly could be.

But with the coming of the tractor, of electricity, of new methods of farming, the scene changed. Today, the farmer relies on millions of other people for the goods and services he needs to operate his farm. He must have these goods to make his living—and he must pay for them in cash. In 1910 the cost of a two-plow tractor would have financed the production expenses of an average United States farm for three and one half years. Today it would run the same farm only six months. And here's why:

[3] From "What Price Plenty?" pamphlet. National Farmers Union. 1575 Sherman Street. Denver, Colorado. 1954. p61-5. Reprinted by permission.

United States farmers today need each year—

Seven million tons of finished steel—more than is used for a year's output of passenger cars.

Fifty million tons of chemical materials—five times the amount farmers used in 1935.

Sixteen and one half billion gallons of crude petroleum— more than is used by any other industry.

Three hundred and twenty million pounds of raw rubber— enough rubber to put tires on six million automobiles.

Fifteen billion kilowatt hours of electric power—enough to supply Chicago, Detroit, Baltimore and Houston for one year.

All of these cost money, but without them farmers could not grow as much food without having more acres. So it would seem that the nation's food supply depends upon the soil and the ability of farmers to pay for the steel, chemicals, fuel and power they need to keep growing enough food to feed our increasing population.

Where does the farmer get the money to pay for his tractors, seed, electricity and fuel? From the price he receives for the crops and livestock he grows. But what assures the farmer that he will receive a fair price for his time, his investment and his labor? Suppose he produces too much food in one year, more food than is needed? And suppose the price drops far below what it cost the farmer to produce it? How does he raise the money necessary to plant and harvest his crop the following year?

Most people will agree that we can get along without many things, but we can't get along without food. Therefore, back in the 1930's, the Government decided to establish a floor below which the price of farm products could not fall. This floor is known as the price support program. It now applies to a few of the so-called basic commodities—corn, wheat, rice, cotton, tobacco and peanuts. The price support program has also been applied to other commodities such as milk products, feed grains and sorghums.

In view of our steadily increasing population, and in view of our long-range needs of 40 per cent more food production by 1975, the farmer must continually plan for abundant production each year. He has to gamble against the risk of weather and price. Sometimes farmers produce more than the nation needs for any given year. Sometimes they produce less. It is impossible to produce "just enough" food.

Here . . . price supports come in. They enable the farmer to get a fair price for his crop regardless of how much he produces. Without price supports, let's suppose that the farmer produced a bumper crop of corn two years in succession. Part of the first year's crop wasn't needed right then, so it was bought at the prevailing low price and stored by private firms. But when the second bumper crop came along it had to compete with last year's crop in the market place. Down went the price and out of business went the farmer.

But suppose price supports were in effect—as they now are. The farmer produces a bumper crop two years in succession. He gets a guaranteed price for his crop the first year, and also the second year. The nation then has in reserve all of the corn that it did not use up in those two years.

But the year after those two bumper crops there is a serious drought. Very little corn is harvested. But the nation does not lack corn because it has wisely stored up reserves to be used for just such an emergency. The Government has bought corn from the farmers in the two years of bumper crops. Now it can sell those reserves to make up for the crop failure of the third year. . . .

A depression can be avoided if labor, industry, Government and agriculture act wisely and cooperatively. Here, it would seem that Government action is sorely needed. By setting price supports at 100 per cent of a fair price—or parity—for all family farm produced commodities, the farmer would be assured of an income. He could then buy the tractors, the power, the fuel that he needs in order to achieve abundant production. The factories would have to employ men to make the tractors. In turn these men would provide a market for the food the farmer produces.

The circle can work both ways. But for an economy of abundance, there has to be cooperative action. Each segment of our economy—industry, labor and agriculture—is so closely related that one cannot long endure if another is at the bottom of the economic mire. There is a saying, which was proved true in the thirties, that depressions are farm fed and farm led. The same is true of prosperity.

FAILURE OF RIGID SUPPORTS [4]

Support at 90 per cent of parity was supposed to boost agricultural production to the limit in view of an insatiable demand abroad and at home during the war and postwar emergency; it was never meant to be a feasible policy for a peacetime economy. As a matter of fact, the 90 per cent support policy did not come into play during the war and immediately thereafter, since demand lifted prices above the support levels.

As the surplus situation proves, rigid price support amounts to price-fixing at the support level, misdirects the use of agricultural resources by maintaining an excess output, prohibits the proper flow of commodities into consumption, attracts additional imports of the goods in surplus, and prices American products out of the world market. . . .

Freely moving prices of farm crops at present in surplus supply would, without public interference, automatically seek a lower level and move the surplus into domestic consumption and export markets. By changing price relations they would induce the farmers to make the necessary adjustments in production through shifting land to more profitable crops.

Rigid supports prevent prices from attaining that lower level and thereby the wrong price signals are issued to all parties concerned on the supply and demand side of the market. The more the level of support deviates from the equilibrium level, the worse the results of the wrong price signals will be. The most

[4] From "Farm Price Supports—Rigid or Flexible?" pamphlet by Karl Brandt, associate director, Food Research Institute, Stanford University. (National Economic Problems no452). American Enterprise Association. 1012 Fourteenth St. Washington 5, D.C. 1954. p6-10, 13-18. Reprinted by permission.

visible and disturbing result is the continuation of excessive production and unmanageable surplus stocks.

If price support remains fixed at 90 per cent of parity, the Government must force the farmers to reduce the output of commodities which are in excess supply by acreage allotments and marketing quotas. On June 19, 1954, for example, Secretary of Agriculture Benson announced what have been characterized as the most drastic agricultural controls in the history of the country. The number of acres which now may be planted to wheat is set at 55 million as contrasted to 78 million in 1952. Under certain circumstances a farmer may be required to submit to a "total acreage allotment" or lose price support on all other crops.

For some crops, acreage allotments alone leave enough leeway for maintaining a high output on fewer acres by intensification and higher yields. Hence output-boosting high rigid price supports require strictly enforced marketing quotas either alone or in addition to acreage allotments. Such interference with managerial decisions on over 5 million farms throughout the nation with uniform percentage quotas is a costly and wasteful substitute for voluntary individual land-use adjustments under the guidance of prices.

Maintenance of 90 per cent support requires an elaborate control administration and enforcement restrictions which tend to freeze crops to their historical location. Aside from the cost in money and manpower involved, it limits the farmers' managerial freedom and transfers the responsibility from the individual to the Government—from the economic to the political sphere. Flexible prices are the only device by which an economic system can combine freedom of enterprise, efficiency, and self-adjustment. To rely chiefly on Government enforcement of quotas and price-fixing is the antithesis of a free-enterprise economy.

The opportunity for farmers to earn an increasing income depends primarily on the purchasing power of the rising number of consumers. A high consumer income requires success in the foreign economic policies of the United States, particularly in foreign trade. Rigid supports of farm prices which lift them above the world-market level make exports of farm products very difficult if not dependent upon practices which amount to

dumping and lead to retaliation by other nations. Export subsidies, two-price systems, give-away programs (except disaster
relief) all fall under policies which are in conflict with the free
multilateral foreign-trade policy to which we adhere. . . .

The change to flexible sliding-scale support prices would
affect primarily the basic commodities. Reduced prices would
create an incentive to reduce output of these surplus commodities and to divert land to other crops. . . .

There is considerable vagueness concerning the aims, the
potential range of success, and the limitations of possible
achievements of the farm price-support policy. Among those
who believe in the maintenance of a strong, self-adjusting free-
enterprise agriculture which keeps the use of food and fiber
resources in balance with the growing industrial economy, there
is basic agreement about the limitations of farm price supports.
They realize that the rising purchasing power of a growing
population basically creates an opportunity for the farmer to
earn an equitable income insofar as he responds in volume and
quality and with the competent use of improved technology to
the consumer's preference as expressed in prices. They also
know that Government price supports can do no more than
cushion the impact upon farm income of a sudden decline in
demand or an excess supply. All who believe in the free-
enterprise economy are aware of the fact that flexible prices are
not only the effect of the forces of supply and demand but,
at the same time, are the causative force that stimulates adjustment on all sides of the market. Fixed prices create surpluses,
flexible prices dispose of them. . . .

Critics of the competitive market economy assert that prices
are ineffective in allocating agricultural resources and propose
that the Government guarantee full parity income to farmers.
Full controls on production and marketing would enforce 100
per cent parity prices. Existing surpluses would be disposed of
by expanding foreign aid to the underfed of the world. They
belittle the concomitant of that policy: the exchange of free-
doms of farm management for Government regimentation and
control.

Stabilization at the war-record levels . . . is impossible under any conceivable program. Since the accumulation of surpluses must be halted and reversed, a temporary adjustment to a somewhat lower gross income is unavoidable. . . .

The present farm price support policy is a residue of the war and postwar emergencies. It ought not to be maintained any longer. Its rigid support at too high a level provides such continued incentive to overproduction that huge, unmanageable excess stocks of commodities are piling up in public granaries. Their maintenance and eventual disposal involves an appalling waste of economic resources and public funds. Unless the incentive to create excess production is gradually diminished by a shift to flexible supports and the adoption of lower modernized parity for all support commodities, the self-adjusting system of free enterprise in agriculture will have to be replaced by production and marketing quotas. Quota systems stagnate our dynamic and creative agricultural economy, which gave such a brilliant account of itself during the war and afterward. The capacity of our 2 million commercial farms to produce is strong and elastic enough to assure the nation of all food requirements even in the event of war. Maintenance of nuisance stocks that clog all normal storage channels and distort the free utilization of our great food resources will, in the long run, reduce the defense potential of American agriculture.

Once the necessary adjustment in the price support policy is made and surpluses are gradually channeled into foreign and domestic consumption, the American farmer will again earn an equitable income based on managerial efficiency and productivity of labor—so long as the industrial economy keeps up a healthy pace of activity and growth—without exorbitant burdens upon all consumers.

DEFECTS IN SUPPORT POLICIES [5]

As the chief means of helping agriculture solve its problems, the Government has for years relied on supporting farm

[5] From "Economic Policy for American Agriculture," pamphlet. Committee for Economic Development, Research and Policy Committee. 444 Madison Avenue. New York 22. January 1956. p 16-18. Reprinted by permission.

prices at a high level. The shortcomings of this approach are illustrated by the ever increasing surpluses accumulated at heavy Government expense. On the other hand, it is sometimes proposed that agricultural prices be left to fluctuate freely in response to every shift of the market. This, too, would create grave problems, as experience shows. A closer look at each of these policies will assist in the search for solutions.

We believe that there are basic defects in the high rigid price support approach. It is a wasteful and, over any long period, a relatively ineffective way of trying to raise the income of the individual farmer.

High level price supports have a tendency to be self-defeating. In part this is because the supports lead to accumulated surpluses, a marked increase in Federal expenditures on subsidies, or both. In any event, efforts will be made by Government to reduce the accumulation of surpluses or the rise in subsidy expenditures by trying to limit output through acreage controls and marketing quotas. If successful, this reduces farm incomes.

There are other reasons why high price supports are an ineffective way of increasing the incomes of individual farmers. A large part of the Government's outlay for purchase of farm commodities merely repays the farmer's costs of producing those commodities and is not reflected in greater net income retained by the farm operators.

In addition, to the extent that net incomes are temporarily increased by this method, two other influences become operative. First, fewer young people would leave agriculture and the adjustment of the farm labor force to an appropriate level at some future time would be made much more difficult. Any temporary gain in farm incomes could well be offset by greater difficulties that would have to be faced later. Second, to the extent that net farm incomes are increased by high price supports, farm land prices will increase. While this increase would benefit existing owners of land, new farmers who must pay the higher prices for the land would gain little from the supports. One of the reasons why farmers in the Great Plains find it difficult to adjust to lower wheat prices is that land values are based on the recent high price supports for wheat.

There are other grave defects in a policy of high level supports. The acreage allotments and marketing quotas that are required lead to inefficiency in production. Areas with expanding output are cut back more than other areas. Individual farmers cannot utilize their own land and labor most efficiently when they must follow arbitrary limitations on the amount of a given crop that may be planted.

Furthermore, acreage allotments and marketing quotas turn out in practice to be weak defenses against mounting production. Farmers often succeed in increasing output even on the smaller acreage allowed them. And though the acreage devoted to cotton or wheat may be restricted, the so-called diverted acres are used for other crops. Little land would be withdrawn from production or transferred to lower yielding uses such as pastures. Thus high cotton and wheat supports, even accompanied by acreage allotments, encourage the maintenance of land in crop production and thereby actually delay a solution of the surplus problem.

We believe that high level price supports have been given an adequate trial and have been found wanting. They have aggravated the surplus problem. High price supports made some contribution to the problem of instability, but at considerable cost to the taxpayer. Low income farmers get no real assistance from high price supports. . . . These failures make it necessary to look further for solutions. . . .

An economy that depends largely upon free markets is more productive than an economy with similar resources that relies upon other mechanisms for directing the use of productive resources.

The movement of particular prices tends to induce more production of things that people want more, and more consumption of things that producers are turning out in increasing volume. For example, if the demand for a particular product declines, its price will decline relative to other prices. This will cause labor and other resources to shift into producing things for which there is a greater demand; at the same time, while the shift is going on, the lower prices will induce consumers to buy more of the large supply, preventing it from going to waste.

In a large and complex economy there is no effective alternative to the price mechanism for keeping production and use efficiently geared together. As a result there must be a clear and commanding reason before we prevent prices from reacting freely to long-range changes in market conditions.

While we cannot dispense with free prices in the operation of our agricultural economy, it appears that, for special reasons, price fluctuations in agricultural markets are much larger than are needed for the efficient balancing of production and consumption. These special reasons are:

First, the production process takes a considerable period of time and once it is started there is little possibility of stopping it. Farmers must attempt to estimate prices several months ahead in making their production decisions. If these estimates turn out to be wrong and many have guessed the same way, either too much or too little will be produced. And prices will either be quite low or quite high—higher or lower than needed to get a correction of production plans.

Second, the farmer cannot accurately predict how much output he will get from a given production process. Many things are beyond his control—for example, rainfall, temperature, evaporation rate, and diseases. Since some of these factors change in a similar manner over a wide area, there is considerable variability from year to year in the national output of wheat or corn or cotton, even when the acreage planted is held constant. When conditions are favorable over a wide geographic area, output is likely to be quite large. And in the case of most crops, a large output usually brings a smaller total income than a small output.

Third, consumers do not change their consumption patterns rapidly in response to small changes in prices for foods and fibers. Thus, in the case of many farm products, relatively small changes in available supplies result in large changes in prices in the opposite direction. At times this result is favorable to farmers; at times it is not. But in any case it adds a large element of uncertainty and instability to farm prices.

Completely free market prices for agricultural products would, of course, end Government-held surpluses altogether, but at excessive costs for producers of some commodities; instability of income would be increased; low income farmers would continue to suffer from lack of adequate land and capital per capita.

We do not believe we can return to a completely free market price situation for agriculture without exposing farmers to unnecessary risks and instability. But we wish to emphasize that a satisfactory farm price policy must retain as many of the desirable features of a freely functioning price system as is possible. Thus, changes in consumer tastes or in the relative costs of producing different farm products should be rather quickly reflected in the market prices. The general level of farm prices should not depart for any considerable length of time from the level that would prevail in a free market in the absence of Government regulation or accumulation of stocks of farm commodities. If such a departure occurs, certain undesirable consequences are inevitable—surpluses accumulate, production restrictions are imposed, and consumer preferences are not effectively registered.

WHERE YOUR FOOD DOLLARS GO [6]

In 1953 farmers received on the average about 45 cents of each dollar that city consumers spent for food products in retail stores. The remaining 55 cents was the share for marketing— including transportation, storage, processing and distribution. Part of these costs went to pay the 5 million workers it took to move these products from the farms to the consumer.

How the food dollar is shared varies widely by commodities and commodity groups. For example, farmers in 1953 averaged 69 cents of each dollar consumers spent for poultry and eggs. They averaged only 22 cents of each dollar spent for grain products such as bread, crackers, and breakfast cereals. . . .

Some products require more marketing services than others. Some are in forms that are very different from the products as they leave the farm. . . .

You, the consumer, do not buy wheat. You buy bread and bakery goods. The bread contains ingredients besides the flour

[6] From "The Farmer's Share of the Food Dollar," leaflet by Kenneth E. Ogren, agricultural economist, Agricultural Marketing Service, United States Department of Agriculture. (Leaflet no 123) Superintendent of Documents. Washington 25, D.C. October 1954. p 1-8.

made from the wheat. You are buying these, and buying also the services of millers, bakers and distributors that go into the production and distribution of the finished goods.

You do not buy cattle. You buy only a piece of the animal after it has been slaughtered and processed and prepared for you in the cuts you prefer. Since people prefer the best, you find the less desirable cuts available at lower prices.

You . . . also are buying many services that formerly were performed in the home. . . .

A recent study by home economists of the Department [of Agriculture] revealed that a family meal of ready-to-serve food costs over one third more than a meal requiring a maximum of home preparation. . . .

The trend toward more commercial preparation is likely to continue, particularly when consumers have a high level of income. As incomes increase, consumers are willing to pay for services that maintain quality and increase the convenience and attractiveness of food products, that save time, and that provide a greater variety of foods.

Consumers in 1953 spent a larger proportion of their income for food than they did before World War II, even though incomes had risen more than food prices. They spent a larger proportion partly because they bought more processed and ready-to-serve foods.

The share that you, the farmer, receive of the consumer's food dollar is computed by comparing the retail cost and the farm value of a typical "market basket" of farm foods bought by a city workingman's family. This "market basket" contains the estimated quantities of all farm-produced food products bought for consumption at home per urban wage-earner and clerical-worker family in 1952. . . .

But the money spent for this market basket of foods is not all the money these families put into food. Not included are expenditures for imported and nonfarm foods such as bananas, canned pineapple, coffee, and fish, and for foods bought in restaurants.

Note, too, that an estimated one sixth of all food is bought by consumers in restaurants. These foods are not included in the typical "market basket." If they were included, you, the

farmer, would find that you get less than 45 cents of the consumer's food dollar. . . .

In 1953, consumers paid out, on the average, $1,002 for a
family "market basket" of food. This was a little less than consumers paid in either of the two preceding years, but more than
in any other year since World War II.

In 1953, farmers received, on the average, $452 for the
produce going into this food basket. This amount was less than
in either of the two preceding years, but well above the prewar
annual average.

And in making comparisons between farm value and retail
cost, we must allow for the portion of the products that does
not go into food. For example, from each one hundred pounds
of live-weight steer, less than half this weight is obtained in
salable retail cuts. This means that even before any marketing
charges are added to the price farmers receive, the price per
pound of the retail cuts is more than double the price obtained
for the live steer.

The difference between the retail cost and the farm value of
the "market basket" is the total marketing margin. It represents all charges made by marketing agencies from the sale of
crops, livestock, or livestock products by the farmer up to the
purchase of food products at retail by the consumer. In 1953,
this marketing margin, or farm-retail price spread, took $550
of the total market-basket value of $1,002. . . .

Wages and salaries are the largest single item in the total
expenses of most food-marketing firms. In the years immediately
preceding 1954, the cost of labor amounted to about 50 per cent
of the total marketing margin. . . .

The increasing importance of marketing services in relation
to farm production is illustrated by shifts in the number of workers in agriculture and in marketing. During the twenty years
ended in 1953, the number of workers in agriculture dropped by
about 30 per cent while the number engaged in food marketing
increased by more than 50 per cent. . . .

In 1939 [middlemen's] profits amounted to 8 per cent of
the total food marketing bill and about 5 per cent of the consumer's food dollar. Earnings statements of large food-proces-

sing companies and retail food chains indicate that for several years before 1954 their profits (before deducting income taxes) per dollar of sales were about the same as, or less than, in 1939. When the higher income-tax rates of those years are considered, net returns per dollar of sales were substantially lower than in prewar years.

A typical supermarket has a profit of about 2 cents per dollar of sales. After deductions for income taxes, this is equal to about 1 cent. Profits per dollar of sales of food manufacturers average somewhat higher although they vary considerably by type of product.

Profits per dollar of sales do not in themselves indicate whether profits of middlemen are too high or too low. . . . We must consider rates of returns on invested capital in marketing firms in relation to returns on invested capital in other comparable industries. A food-marketing firm with a low profit per dollar of sales could be receiving a high rate of profit in relation to its total investment. But it is clear that profits are not a major proportion of the total marketing margin. If any substantial savings in over-all marketing margins for farm food products in general are to be realized, reductions must be made in operating costs. . . .

The consumer's food costs include marketing costs along with what the farmer receives. The marketing cost or margin is determined by factors that differ widely from those that affect prices of farm products. For example, when the farmer's price for his product declines because of a bigger supply, this does not directly or immediately reduce the costs of marketing. These costs, like rent and taxes and wages, tend to hold steady. For that reason, marketing margins usually vary less than farmers' prices, especially percentagewise. This is particularly noticeable in periods when farm prices are declining.

Some of the larger costs in marketing are slow to change. Items like rent, freight rates, utilities, and wage rates may be definitely fixed by individual contracts or Government regulations. They are not immediately affected by either inflationary or deflationary pressures. In an inflation, both farm prices and marketing margins rise, but the marketing margin goes up more slowly than farm prices. However, the rise in farm prices lasts for a shorter time than the advance in marketing costs.

The cost items in the marketing margin are more inflexible when prices fall than when they rise. The rigidities of these costs have prevented substantial declines in the marketing margin when farm prices have fallen as a result of weakening demand or increasing supplies. Since World War I, marketing margins declined substantially only during the severe deflations of 1920-21 and the early thirties. Even during these periods, the reduction in margins was slower and considerably smaller than the decline in farm prices.

During the years 1946 through 1953, almost all costs of marketing increased. Services to consumers were expanded, as with prepared foods. Rents and utility costs went up. Local, state, and Federal taxes increased, widening the margin between farm and retail prices. Hourly earnings of employees in food marketing rose more than 80 per cent. They were still rising in early 1954 along with those in other industries. Eleven general increases in rail freight rates since World War II had been authorized by the Interstate Commerce Commission. Railroad freight rates for agricultural commodities rose 65 per cent between 1945 and 1953.

Although they rise more slowly than farmers' prices, costs of these kinds tend to resist downward pressures. Marketing agencies have no direct control over many of the charges.

However, there are inefficiencies in the marketing process, just as in everything else. Marketing margins can be lowered by pinpointing these inefficiencies, exploring through research the ways to overcome them, and carrying out a practical program to encourage adoption of improved methods.

Part of the variation in the farmer's share of the consumer's food dollar reflects changes in price trends in the economy as a whole. More important to the farmer than the share he gets of the food dollar are the returns he receives in relation to his production costs. But the total income farmers get is greatly influenced by the size of the marketing margin or the spread between farm and retail prices.

IV. SURPLUSES

EDITOR'S INTRODUCTION

Discussion of surpluses of price-supported agricultural products strikes at the root of the ailments besetting the American farmer: that he produces more than consumers can or will buy at prices yielding him a fair return.

In "Too Much Is Our Trouble," a magazine editor analyzes this ironic dilemma. Two agricultural economists discuss whether a growing population will solve our surplus problem and whether, on the other hand, our farm production will keep pace with population growth.

A Study Committee on Federal Aid to Agriculture reports on possibilities of expanding domestic markets and better national farm distribution. A farm editor calls for intensive advertising-promotion efforts to sell our people more agricultural products.

A business magazine writer reviews the Government's efforts to expand foreign markets. Another farm editor calls attention to opportunities in this direction. An agricultural economist weighs the problems and pitfalls of foreign agricultural sales.

TOO MUCH IS OUR TROUBLE [1]

What is our surplus problem? In most countries an agricultural surplus would be that part of production which is not used; in the United States, as a result of our Federal price-support program, a surplus is that part of production which will not return a reasonable profit to the producer through the normal channels of trade. . . . An ordinary surplus is usually waste and is seldom repeated. The American-type surplus in basic farm commodities is subsequently acquired and stored by the Government. As of this 1955 spring, our Commodity Credit Corpora-

[1] From an article by Richard Thruelsen, associate editor, *Saturday Evening Post.* *Saturday Evening Post.* 227:30+. June 18, 1955. Reprinted by permission.

tion has $7.5 billion in public funds invested in surplus commodities. This means that every adult American—and there are approximately 100 million of us—has a $75 stake in an agricultural surplus which, for the most part, we can't eat, we can't wear, we can't sell and we can't give away.

This astonishing total of too much is not simply a bookkeeping entry. In the case of the $4 billion worth of surplus we already have on hand, the bill has been paid in hard cash to the farmers; the other $3.5 billion is represented by loan commitments which must be honored by the Government—also in hard cash. And to this whopping bill must be added the $1 million a day we pay to store the crops we don't want and can't use. . . .

What factors have combined to produce this flood of unwanted food and fiber during a period when our domestic consumption has been at an all-time high? The simple answer, of course, is overproduction—though the reasons for the overproduction are not simple. The increased skill of our farmers, the development of hybrid strains and new fertilizers and pest controls, and the widespread mechanization of farm operations have all tended to increase production in the basic commodities during a period when our farm population has dwindled by a third. Indeed, the five-fold increase of farm tractors since 1940 has not only spurred production; it has also eliminated 85 per cent of the feed-grain market once represented by the horses and the mules which worked the farms.

To these improvements in the production cycle must be added the partial loss of our foreign markets. Reasons: our former customers are becoming more self-sufficient or they lack the dollars to buy our products when they do need them—a part of the penalty we pay for having become a creditor nation. Though our foreign aid programs have siphoned dollars abroad and ameliorated this situation somewhat, we have nevertheless seen our annual agricultural exports decline by almost $1 billion in the last eight years. . . .

A steady increase in national income has revolutionized this country's eating habits; we now eat far more meat, eggs, fruits and vegetables and far less flour and cereal products per capita than we did a quarter of a century ago. Cotton, another of our basic surpluses, has faced a similar contraction of its market through the development of synthetic fibers.

What happened to that good old law of supply and demand? . . . Why . . . has it not worked with the so-called basic commodities which are producing the surpluses?

The answer lies in a strange modification of economic law called price supports—a device by which the Government has guaranteed a fixed minimum return to the producers of the basic farm commodities for the last two decades. . . .

One of the most generally accepted features of the whole price support, surplus buying program is that it helps the farmers. We have been educated to accept as a fact the idea that farmers, as a class, need Federal financial aid. Let's see how that premise stands up. In the first place, more than half of our 5.5 million farm operators either do not produce any of the basic commodities which account for nine tenths of our surplus or produce such small quantities that price support payments mean very little to them. Or, to put it another way, commodities receiving no price support represent 54 per cent of the United States cash farm income; commodities receiving flexible support (before the present law was enacted) represented 20 per cent of the farm cash income, and the high-support commodities represented 26 per cent of the farmers' cash income. From this it is plain that farm legislation which encourages surpluses does help farmers—but only some of them. . . .

A Department of Agriculture economist has established the fact that the per capita net assets of our 22 million farm population—that is, the debt-free wealth of each man, woman and child—now averages $13,000. If, as the Administration recently stated, there are 1.5 million farm families with extremely low incomes, this astounding figure suggests that the fortunate majority of our farm population is decidedly prosperous.

And now let us take a look at this part of our farm population that receives the high-support aid and is the primary producer of our surplus.

In Missouri the average loan to all cotton farmers on their 1953 crops was $395. The average of the five largest loans was $153,191. In California one busy farmer . . . received a Government loan of over $1 million for raising cotton for which there was no market. In Minnesota the average corn loan was $1,843; the largest corn loan was $73,049. In North Dakota the average wheat loan was $2,890; the average of the five largest wheat loans was $71,246. In Alabama five cotton growers received loans totaling $503,559.59—as against the state's average cotton loan of $318.45.

From this brief glance at the loan figures, it is plain that . . . the large payments went to agricultural big businesses which produce vast quantities of commodities that have no immediate market. A farmer who received a Government loan of $71,253 on his 1954 wheat crop, for instance, would have to be working some 2,000 acres—which is quite a farm. How much Federal financial aid such an entrepreneur needs might be a matter of debate. . . .

This may suggest a question: Is "loan" or "payment" the right word here? For if these are loans, they may be repaid with interest and the Government's investment in that particular piece of surplus would then turn out to be nothing more than a book-keeping transaction. The answer is that the terms are generally interchangeable—the loan is more often than not a payment for the commodity involved.

An example in wheat will illustrate the method by which the Government acquires the surplus. A wheat farmer in 1954 harvested 1,000 bushels of wheat, working within the price support, acreage allotment, marketing quota plan; he had the county field inspector sample and measure his grain and subsequently procured a price support loan (from a local bank approved by the CCC) of $2,240 at the loan rate of $2.24 per bushel based on the 90 per cent of parity at which the Department of Agriculture supported the crop. When the loan matured a few months later the farmer could have (1) paid it off, plus 3.5 per cent interest, and taken back his wheat and sold it in the open market or (2) kept the $2,240 and let the CCC satisfy the loan at the local bank and take the wheat. Since the loan rate, for some years, has been at 90 per cent of parity and the open-market price of wheat last year averaged only 82 per cent of parity—partly because of the depressive influence of the huge surplus—the farmer generally kept the cash and let the wheat go into the Government storage bins—which added to the surplus, which further depressed the market price, and so on.

That $1 million-a-day bill the American taxpayer is footing to store the surpluses of wheat, corn, cotton, dairy products and the several score other commodities is spent in many ways in many parts of the country. Butter and cheese are stored in rented, commercial cold-storage facilities in the Midwest and in the New York City area. Wheat is stored in rented elevators, CCC-owned bins, in tents, and in 317 idle Maritime Administration ships. Corn is stored in CCC-owned facilities in the corn belt, and cotton is warehoused in the southern states. Though some of these items, such as cotton and wool and turpentine, can be held in storage indefinitely, no one knows just how long some commodities such as butter and wheat and corn will retain their functional food values. Experts hazard a guess that wheat is good for five to seven years under correct storage conditions. For this reason the possibility of spoilage must be added to the factors of fire, theft and waste which weight the storage bill.

The Commodity Credit Corporation, which is responsible for disposing of the surplus, managed to unload products valued at $1.4 billion (out of an inventory valued at more than $4 billion) during the calendar year of 1954. That $1.4 billion distribution of 1954 surplus does not mean that the taxpayer was taken off the hook for that much—for during the fiscal year ending June 1954, the CCC lost more than $400 million on its price support—that is, surplus—operations. In other words, the past year has seen more surpluses accumulating, more surpluses distributed and more losses through both operations.

What can we do with these mountains of food and fiber which are pushing us slowly along the path to the poorhouse? . . . There are always some domestic commercial sales from surplus because some wholesale distributors let the Government take over a part of their former role as purchaser and warehouser of commodities for future marketing; as a middleman in the wheat business, for instance, the CCC last year had a hand in moving about 5 per cent of our annual consumption from surplus storage to American stomachs. In general, however, surpluses can't be used domestically because it would wreck the regular markets.

The same reason, with added international considerations, prevents the CCC from dumping surplus stocks abroad. Flooding foreign markets with our surplus would not only endanger our own regular export programs in the various commodities, it would also demoralize the world markets and endanger the economies of other friendly exporting countries. Last year our commercial exports from surplus totaled $500 million—about one thirteenth of what we then had on hand.

Noncommercial sales to foreign governments and relief societies, transfers to the Foreign Operations Administration, veterans' hospitals and our armed forces, donations to foreign and domestic school-lunch programs and barter deals in which we trade surplus for strategic materials, all accounted for another mighty trickle—about $400 million worth—from our stockpile last year. In each case the CCC has to be wary lest it tread on sensitive toes; the French dairy industry protests American donations of butter to its school-lunch program because this will mean that the tots will eat less French butter at dinner, while American commission merchants and the producer groups raise a howl if they think the armed forces are dipping into free surplus stocks when they should be buying current-production butter. And if some nation does accept a donation of say, 2 million tons of our surplus wheat—as India did, for family relief—the CCC must dig deep for the expenses of transporting the gift overseas.

The last Congress, at the request of the Administration, passed two laws which will ease the tension as the CCC's borrowing authority—now $10 billion—is boosted higher and higher. One of these legislative aids allows the Department of Agriculture to accept foreign currencies for surplus stocks—giving dollar-short countries a trading medium. The foreign money will be used to pay for our offshore commitments.

The second legislative prop for the CCC disposal program is the Administration's recently announced $2.5 billion "set-aside" provision, which earmarks that amount of the surplus as a sort of strategic reserve. This gargantuan piece of bookkeeping merely recognizes a potential always implicit in the surplus—that in the event of a disaster which flattened our basic crops, the country would have enough stored reserve to ride out a year. The "set-aside" does not affect the surplus problem by a bale or a bushel—actually, by decreasing the "available" inventory, this move will raise the level of supports under the new, flexible price support program. . . .

There are a number of ideas on how the tide of too much can be slowed or stopped. Some optimists hold that our expected population gain—200 million plus by 1970—will enable us to eat our way to a balanced production. Unfortunately, recent world figures show that agricultural production is out-pacing population growth—a contradiction of the Malthusian doctrine. Another school believes that turning more grain into meat and dairy products—a process by which you shrink the food potential of each acre planted to grain—would cut the flow of unwanted corn and wheat. This in turn would mean substantial changes in the price structure of the grain markets—a possibility which already has the wheat and corn states squaring off against one another in Congress. A few Washington economists suggest that we simply pay the farmers not to produce—pointing out that we could pull 40 million acres out of production for what we are spending on our current surplus-purchase program. This desperate remedy is another form of the Henry Wallace plow-it-under program. . . .

A more conservative group in Washington and the farm states hope that the current trend toward lower, flexible price supports and more radical acreage allotment cuts will slowly turn the tide. . . . There also have been suggestions that limitations be placed on individual loans under the price support system. This restriction-of-benefits device was incorporated in the . . . short-lived Brannan Plan—which proposed, in effect, to guarantee every cooperating farmer a tax-paid annual wage of not more than $2,500. Whatever the virtues of such a limitation, it is hard to see how you can penalize bigness and efficiency in a democracy—or how you could make the limitations stick.

Some solution for practical production control may germinate from these suggestions. As for that $7.5 billion surplus we'll have on hand and the end of this year [1955]—well, the CCC is ready and willing to listen to any new suggestions.

CAN WE EAT UP OUR SURPLUSES? [2]

One suggestion is that we could reduce or eliminate our agricultural surpluses by expanding domestic food consumption. The suggestion takes two forms:

1. We have needy families that are not eating enough food. If ways could be found to expand their food consumption, surplus food stocks would be reduced or eliminated.

2. Most consumers would like to eat more animal products. If ways could be found to increase consumption of these products, which use up more resources per pound than cereal foods, for instance, the surplus problem would be solved.

These are the suggestions; how do they stack up?

The nutritive quality of diet of low-income families, as well as the average diet in this country, has improved over the last twenty years. Large groups of the population no longer have very poor diets, and frank dietary deficiency diseases are rare. This improvement has not come about as a result of our eating more food. The annual per capita consumption of food measured in pounds stood at 1,542 in 1930, fell to 1,494 in 1934, rose to 1,674 in 1945, and slipped back to 1,530 in 1952. This is a remarkably stable pattern, considering the dramatic economic changes that took place over this period.

The nutritional quality of the American diet has improved because the composition of the diet has improved. The composition improved because of the general improvement in economic conditions, the enrichment and fortification of foods, and the spread of popular education in nutrition. . . . Low-income families still are not eating as much of some foods as they would like, and many of these foods make important contributions to the nutritive content of the diet. . . .

One way to increase the consumption of food would be to discontinue price supports and let prices seek their own levels in

[2] From "Surplus Disposal and Domestic Market Expansion," by Geoffrey S. Shepherd, professor of agricultural economics, Iowa State College. In *United States Agriculture: Perspectives and Prospects*; background papers and final report of Seventh American Assembly, Harriman, New York, May 5-8, 1955. The Assembly. Columbia University. New York 27. 1955. p69-77. Reprinted by permission.

the open market. At these lower prices, the surpluses would move into consumption.

This would not necessarily throw farmers to the mercies of the open market. The principle of price supports could be retained, by setting "support" levels as before, but making up the difference between those levels and open-market prices by direct payments to farmers. . . .

On the face of it, this makes better economic sense than the present program of supporting prices and accumulating surpluses. The present program hits consumers two or three times over—once in high prices, and again in high taxes, and again in reduced production and consumption.

A program of direct payments would cost no more than the existing program of price supports. For products with inelastic demand, government payments would be higher, but consumer payments for the product would be lower than under the existing program. The total of the two would be the same. And the net benefit would be that consumers would eat up all the product, at lower prices, that now goes to waste in the form of unwanted surpluses.

The big shortcoming of the direct payment program is that it would subsidize consumption for everybody, rich and poor alike. It would waste a lot of public funds. . . .

The greatest nutritional deficiencies are found in the low-income groups, and they are caused chiefly by the low incomes. The sensible thing to do is to increase the food consumption of these groups by lowering the cost of food to them, not to everybody. How can this best be done?

There are two simple ways to subsidize the consumption of food by low-income groups. . . . One way is to give low-income consumers enough money to buy a better diet. The other is to give them food outright.

The trouble with the first way—giving low-income consumers cash to buy food—is that it would become a general relief program, not a straight food program. The 1948 food survey showed that a family with an annual income of $2,000 spent about half of it—$1,000—on food. If you doubled their income, they would not double their expenditures on food. Instead, they would spend only about a third of the total income of $4,000 (that is, $1,333) on food. Thus, of the extra $2,000 they received, they would spend only one sixth ($1,333 — $1,000 = $333) for food. Only one sixth of the "food" money would actually be spent on food, the rest being spent for all sorts of other things.

Perhaps it would be better then to go to the other extreme and give them food outright—just set up distribution depots and give the food away, free.

Strangely enough, distributing food free also would turn out to be a general relief program rather than a straight food program. The reason for this is not as obvious as with the cash program.

Let us consider the $2,000 family again. They could go to the free food store and get for nothing the food they needed for an adequate diet. So, instead of spending half their $2,000 income on food and half on other things, they would not have to spend any on food. They probably would spend most of their income on other things, in about the same proportions as if they were given $1,000 additional cash, as above. So what started out as a subsidy for food would end up as more of a subsidy for other things than for food. This is called the "substitution problem."

In addition, this free food system would have serious political and sociological shortcomings. It would mean setting up an additional food distribution system—a Government system—to compete with the private or regular system. And it would have too much of a connotation of breadlines. . . .

The Food Stamp Program, which was in effect from 1939 to 1943, was an attempt to avoid the shortcomings of both the methods considered above. It provided low-income people with money that could be spent only for food. And it provided them with only enough of this "food money" to cover the cost of an adequate diet. . . .

The prewar Food Stamp Program sold to low-income people orange-colored food stamps for hard cash, dollar for dollar. Along with each $1 worth of these orange-colored stamps it gave

50 cents' worth of blue-colored stamps good only for specified surplus foods.

At first, the surplus list was kept short. But, with the passage of time, more and more products were added until (from December 1939 to June 1940) it included products for which families receiving less than $500 per year ordinarily spent 35 per cent of their total food expenditures, and families receiving $500 to $1,000 ordinarily spent 27 per cent.

Only about 30 per cent of the food stamps was spent for blue-stamp (surplus-list) foods. This does not mean that the blue stamps were 30 per cent effective. If as much as 30 per cent of the food money had been spent for surplus-list foods anyway, it would mean that the blue stamps accomplished nothing. In 1940, low-income families spent from 27 to 35 per cent of their total food expenditures for surplus-list foods. Under those conditions, the blue stamps must have been almost completely ineffective. This conclusion is confirmed by other data, which showed that purchases of blue-stamp foods by participants (expressed as a percentage of total food expenditures) were only about 3 per cent higher than corresponding purchases by nonparticipants. . . .

In the light of experience with the Food Stamp Plan, Senator Aiken introduced a Food Allotment Plan in 1943 and on frequent occasions after that date. His plan . . . sets up a "basic food allotment" per person per week . . . that would provide an adequate diet. It then offers to sell to anybody, for 40 per cent of his income, enough food stamp books to buy this food allotment. This is a feature which solves at one stroke the problem of substitution and the problem of how many and which people to take into the program.

It solves the problem of substitution by taking the money that the participants used to spend for food away from them, so they cannot spend it for other things. And it leaves each man free to decide whether or not to come into the program, on the basis of his income and the size of his family. . . . Families would automatically sort themselves out according to income and number in the family. No administrator would have to decide whom to include and whom to exclude. All that would be required would be a good system of checking on the accuracy of the income statements. . . .

The way to solve surplus problems is not to try desperately to move the surpluses into consumption one way or another while perpetuating their continued production, but to stop producing the surpluses in the first place. And the way to stop producing surpluses is to stop misusing price supports as means of increasing farm incomes.

CAN WE FEED FUTURE GENERATIONS? [3]

Can agriculture's productive capacity meet our future needs? To answer this question we need (1) some idea of how present capacity compares with our current needs, and (2) some idea of what our increased needs may be in the foreseeable future.

It does not take much excess capacity in agriculture to create surplus problems. . . . At the beginning of the last marketing year, our carryovers of wheat were 110 per cent, of cotton 77 per cent, and of corn 29 per cent, of the current year's total consumption and exports. The wheat carryover has built up since 1950 at the rate of 15 per cent, the cotton carryover since 1951 at 15 per cent, and the corn carryover since 1952 at 13 per cent, per year. Over a period of five or six years, we have gotten from four to thirteen months ahead of consumption.

Looked at from a farmer's price-conscious point of view, such carryovers are terrifying. Looked at in historical perspective, our margin of productive capacity over consumption looks comfortable in the short run—about right, given some adjustments among products produced, in view of international tensions and the responsibilities faced by the United States as the leader of the non-Communist world.

Even apart from war fears, however, a longer run point of view sometimes inspires in some people a deep-seated, Malthusian fear that population may again press on our capacity to pro-

[3] From "Agriculture's Technological Revolution," by Glenn L. Johnson, professor of agricultural economics, Michigan State College. In *United States Agriculture: Perspectives and Prospects*; background papers and final report of Seventh American Assembly, Harriman, New York, May 5-8, 1955. The Assembly. Columbia University. New York 27. 1955. p39-41. Reprinted by permission.

duce. . . . Our population is growing at a rate of over 2 million people per year. In mid-1954, we had 162 million. By 1975, there may be well over 200 million mouths to feed, perhaps more than a third again as many people as in 1950. . . .

From 1954 to 1975 output may have to increase 30 per cent —or about as much as output increased from 1930 to date. This calls for at least as rapid (if not more rapid) an increase in production than we have had in recent decades. . . .

[It was] estimated in 1952 that by 1975 we might increase our use of land resources by about 8 per cent. Thus, a major part of the increase in output will have to come from (1) an expanded use of non-land capital and (2) the use of improved technologies. There is little doubt among agriculturalists that the necessary increase in production can be accomplished. . . .

Before additional resources and technology can be used, an individual must be both *able* and (barring the use of police force) *willing* to acquire and use them. Not all farmers have the ability or willingness to acquire more resources. The same is true of technical information. . . .

An agricultural policy aimed at increasing productivity has three main avenues open as far as the use of existing technology is concerned:

1. It may attempt to carry information on technological and organizational possibilities to farmers who are willing and able to (a) invest in resources and (b) absorb and use the technology.

2. It may transfer additional resources to farmers who are unable to acquire them on their own. Such transfers may involve direct transfer of ownership or only aids in borrowing.

3. It may attempt to reform the value systems of farmers who are able but unwilling to acquire and use additional resources and technological information.

EXPANDING DOMESTIC CONSUMPTION [4]

Beginning with the various emergency relief and agricultural assistance programs in 1933, Congress established the principle

[4] From "A Study Committee Report on Federal Aid to Agriculture," submitted to the Commission on Intergovernmental Relations. Superintendent of Documents. Washington 25, D.C. June 1955. p 18-20.

of supporting prices of agricultural commodities by various means, including Federal purchase of commodities in surplus supply and the donation of such surplus commodities to nonprofit school-lunch programs and institutions and to persons and families determined to be in need by state and local welfare agencies. . . .

In fiscal year 1953 $67 million worth of commodities were distributed to the 48 states of which $50 million went to the school-lunch program and $17 million to welfare and charitable purposes. In fiscal year 1954 the non-school-lunch distribution approached $50 million. States receiving donated commodities are required to pay all administrative and handling costs incurred in distributing the commodities within the state. States are not required to contribute matching funds against the value of the commodities.

The Committee accepts without argument the principle that so long as the Federal Government continues to acquire and hold stocks of surplus agricultural commodities, the Federal Government should continue to make them available for consumption—both domestic and foreign—before letting them go to waste.

The Committee views with concern two features which characterize the present program of surplus commodity donations. In the first place the Federal Government is engaged extensively in the physical food-handling business — warehousing, transportation, packaging, repackaging, and accounting for a variety of food stuffs. Also, state and local governments and welfare agencies become similarly involved in the physical aspects of food handling and distribution. Secondly, the "giveaway" concept underlies the relationship between the Federal Government and the states with respect to these commodities. The Committee strongly recommends that additional means be found of disposing of these surplus commodities through regular commercial channels and secondly, that state and local governments be required to make at least token payments against the original cost of the commodities. Specifically the Committee recommends that the United States Department of Agriculture and the Department of Health, Education, and Welfare convene a small committee of representatives of appropriate levels of government and of the

food industry for the purpose of exploring the possibility of instituting a locally operated certificate plan or some other means
of commercial distribution.

For example, if the Department of Agriculture ascertains that
potatoes are to be in surplus supply and that an additional consumption of 1,000 carloads of potatoes during a designated
period of time is necessary to prevent a collapse of the market,
the Department could notify the several states that it was prepared to honor certificates issued for the purchase of potatoes in
an amount not to exceed a certain sum for each state. Based
upon money and quantity allocations from the state government,
local welfare agencies could then issue certificates to their needy
clients for the purchase of designated quantities of potatoes.
These certificates would be taken by the clients to the retail store
and the potatoes obtained. The retail stores would send the certificates back to the United States Department of Agriculture for
reimbursement. Coupled with such a plan the states would transfer funds to the Department of Agriculture to cover a portion of
the cost of the commodities obtained by the welfare clients. (The
money presently expended by the states in the physical transportation and handling of the surplus commodities would go a considerable distance toward making up such a token payment.)
Admittedly such a system is not easy to develop or administer,
and many "bugs" would no doubt develop. Experimentation in
selected areas should precede the nation-wide adoption of any
such certificate or stamp plan.

Assuming token payment by recipient states and private organizations, and pending the shift to distribution through commercial trade channels, the Committee recommends that immediate steps be taken to reduce and eliminate much of the red tape
which currently surrounds the transfer of commodities from
Federal to state custody. Present procedures involve Federal inspection of state warehouses, inventory and accounting records,
and the tracing of commodities from the state receiving point to
the end user. These procedures entail a large volume of inspection, audit and other kinds of paper work. The states have been
receiving the surplus commodities for several years, and whatever
the Federal Government has had to contribute in the way of

technical assistance to states in terms of warehousing and distribution practices should have borne reasonably full fruit by this time. It might be argued by some that certain less efficient states or states whose local units of government are beset by extreme partisanship might misuse and divert the commodities from purposes which were intended by the Congress. It might be further argued that such "backward" states need further Federal assistance in terms of warehousing and good distribution practices. However, it appears to the Committee that the Federal Government should assume reasonable competence and sincerity on the part of the states. Procedures which assume illegal desires of the states to divert or otherwise misuse donated commodities would seem to have no place in the federal system of government as we know it. Consequently, it is recommended that upon introduction of token payments by recipient states, title be considered to pass from the Federal to the state government upon the delivery of commodities to the designated receiving point in the state, and that present Federal inspection, audit, and other policing procedures be discontinued.

As a further interim recommendation, pending further experimentation with commercial distribution, states are urged to designate a single agency to receive surplus commodities and to deal with the United States Department of Agriculture regarding them. All but fourteen of the states have designated a single state agency. States are quick to complain about the multiplicity of Federal agencies. Similar criticism can be directed at those states which require the Federal Government to deal with a variety of state agencies in the conduct of a single program.

SELLING THE FARMER'S PRODUCTS [5]

Secretary Benson stated it, completely and well, in just nine words.

I had asked him: "What, in your opinion, can farmers do to expand the demand for their good farm products, when there are so many other things consumers are tempted to buy?"

[5] From "Agriculture's Next Big Job—Make People Want Farm Products," by Jim Roe, managing editor, Successful Farming. Successful Farming. 53:43+. August 1955. Copyright 1955, Meredith Publishing Company, Des Moines 3, Iowa. Reprinted by permission.

The Secretary's reply: "Agriculture must be competitive—in price, quality, *and promotion*."

We already are competitive in the first two, he explained. But it is in that vital third leg of our stool that we fall far short. Consumers are spending their dollars—which could make short work of our "surpluses"—for other things partly because we haven't asked them to spend those dollars for farm products.

Here and there, when we've tried asking them, they have responded. Dairymen are quite certain their last year's campaign, through the American Dairy Association, sold three billion pounds of milk which would not have been sold otherwise. Our short campaigns on behalf of specific meats have been similarly gratifying.

These pilot-plant "demand expansion" efforts have convinced many agricultural leaders that here indeed is one of agriculture's next big opportunities. Fortunately, all three of our major farm organizations are agreed on this point. And other farm-commodity groups are tooling up to do the job. . . . In Denver, alert cattlemen formed the National Beef Council, whose sole purpose is to make consumers want to eat more beef. . . .

Each of these efforts is aimed—not at merely shifting consumer dollars from one food to another, but at the job of shifting to farm products some of those dollars which are now going to nonfarm goods. This is free enterprise at its purest in action, and it's a mighty fast league. Do we as farmers have a good chance to make our fair share of hits? Most marketing experts, studying the following three questions, vote "Yes!"

Do we have a good product? We are growing and selling the most remarkable products known to man. We are producing products which work miracles. What product other than food can do all these jobs: build pretty girls and strong, healthy, young men; give you "training-table energy" for greater success in your job; give your children a heritage of health which will stand by them all their lives; protect you from many diseases, and make the attack of many others much milder than it otherwise would be; keep you younger, more vigorous, longer; and truly put the "gold" in your "golden years"? These are just some of the miracles good food can perform. We have never adequately explained them.

What is our market potential? For far too long, we have limited our thinking by assuming that the American market for farm products was "just so big." If the manufacturers of non-farm goods had stuck their heads down there in the sand with us, and adopted the same attitude, we would still be a nation of small businessmen. But they didn't. They decided to make people want their products. Farmers must do the same.

We have two opportunities to sell more, besides many opportunities to see to it that America's needy families receive at least a part of their public assistance in the form of food, and wool and cotton clothing.

One of these selling opportunities lies with our increasing population. There are simply going to be more people. Each of them must eat nourishing food and wear adequate clothes.

The other opportunity is to raise the level of United States' nutrition. It is nowhere near as high as our natural American pride leads us to believe. Several large-scale, very recent, studies show an alarming percentage of our population does not eat the food it needs. Their purchasing power is going for other things. Their physical health—and farmers' financial health—will both be improved in great measure if we can win some of that consumer purchasing power back to food and fiber.

Who can do this—and how? Farmers themselves can do it —and must do it. We shall have help, of course, from each branch of industry which works with agriculture. But we must not expect them to do the job alone. We must accept our responsibility—and seize our opportunity—to show what farm products can do for people. Farm-minded, farm-spirited people must do this. No one else has quite the incentive to make sure that it is done. It must be a crusade, not just another job to be done.

If we try, we can make food, cotton, and wool the symbols of gracious American living. In the months ahead in *Successful Farming,* we will explore, together, the ways agriculture has tried this, and the ways in which we might try harder. We can show the American people how our products will make them healthier, happier, more successful in their business and social life. Better yet, each of these stories will be true—we can safely say, "Satisfaction or your money back!"

EXPANDING OVERSEAS MARKETS [6]

The Agricultural Trade Development and Assistance Act passed by the Eighty-third Congress . . . appropriated $700 million to assist private exporters in selling surplus farm products abroad for foreign currencies.

The plan will help bridge the dollar gap between the United States and countries where dollar credits are short. Its main purpose is to cut sizable chunks out of our mountainous pile of surplus farm products and at the same time prevent "dumping." . . .

The Commodity Credit Corporation has on hand enough wheat—743 million bushels—for about a full year's domestic use. Also included in its holdings, but by no means all of them, are 487 million bushels of corn, 2 million pounds of tobacco and 1.8 million bales of cotton.

No one knows how big a hole can be cut in these surpluses by the use of $700 million for sales made in foreign currencies.

Each transaction will be separate, governed by agreements between individual countries and the United States. But it is believed the sales will put a dent in Government inventories.

Under the Act, known as Public Law 480, the Government is by no means the leading performer in the operation. The star role falls to United States exporters and traders who carry out their work through regular private channels of trade. Traders will set the price in competition with farm commodity traders from exporting countries, and the sales will be made by them.

The Government's role is to get the show on the road and to supply the best tools available for the American trader's sales kit. Sound merchandise tailored to the needs and tastes of the customer is the backbone of any selling job. If the product doesn't meet the customer's requirements there's no sense in going on with the sales talk. The Commodity Credit Corporation, which finances price support operations in the Department of Agriculture, can under its own authority prepare commodities for export under Public Law 480 by contracting for repackaging, transportation and other handling costs.

[6] From "Food Surplus Heads Overseas," by Ben James, writer and editor now with the United States Department of Agriculture, Washington, D.C. *Nation's Business.* 43:86-7. February 1955. Copyright 1955. Reprinted from the February issue of *Nation's Business.*

To date the Foreign Agricultural Service, which administers the Department of Agriculture's part in Public Law 480, has helped in the development of programs which may involve more than $450 million.

Many and varied are the jobs that can be done in fitting our agricultural products to the tastes of foreigners. Among them is the repackaging of butter. The Commodity Credit Corporation buys butter for price support purposes in blocks weighing from 60 to 70 pounds. To meet foreign consumption demands these could be repackaged in 1-pound and 1.5-pound prints. Nonfat dry milk, bought by the Commodity Credit Corporation in 150- to 200-pound barrels, could be repacked in 4.5-pound containers for use abroad.

There is a foreign currency market in India, Pakistan and the Far East for our butter providing we convert it into ghee . . . by boiling it until it is comparatively free from moisture. . . . Experiments are now being carried on by American industry to find ways of making American ghee so it is entirely satisfactory to the people of the Far East.

Another effort is under way to create a continuing market for United States farm products and at the same time narrow the dollar gap. This is a move to encourage the investment of American capital in industries in foreign lands that can use American farm commodities as raw materials.

A sample of this type of operation can take the form of plants turning out milk and ice cream made by recombining nonfat dry milk solids and butter oil with water. Five such factories are now furnishing milk to our Army in Japan and vicinity. Such plants can be financed under Public Law 480 by money loaned to native investors who own and operate the plants. Or, if American private capital is invested in these factories, it is possible for the investors to convert their native currency received in their operation into dollars. This can be done only in line with basic agreements drawn up in advance between the two governments concerned.

First reports of Public Law 480 brought objections in this country and abroad that the Act was designed to carry out a vast dumping program that would shatter world agricultural prices and otherwise disrupt, if not destroy, normal channels of trade.

However, the actual working of the Act proves the alarms unfounded. Consider the first agreement signed under the Act with a foreign nation—one with the Turkish government. In this agreement use of the commodity was limited to prevent damage to normal channels of trade. The facts were that Turkey, an exporting nation, suffered a poor wheat crop in 1954. The United States agreed to open surplus wheat for sale through regular trade channels. But the two nations agreed that Turkey could export none of the wheat with the exception of a small lot for which she had already made commitments.

There are a number of circumstances where the employment of our agricultural surplus trade policy, far from carrying a shadow of dumping, can become a boon to the peace of the free world. One such instance would be the use of our foreign currency program in free countries that are now buying farm products from Iron Curtain countries. We may be able to supply these countries at prices competitive with those of the slave countries and in no way affect the channels of trade of the free nations. By so doing we would not only cut off trade from the Soviet bloc but open up new markets for the free world.

Another instance where our surplus commodities may move into nations without disturbance to regular trade occurs in the case where one nation has been dependent upon another particular nation for its supply of a commodity. The supplying nation's source fails for one reason or another. The United States can step into the breach with supplies. Another case, too, is where nations are under rationing because of shortages in farm commodities we can fill in, and in amounts that will relieve the pressure of the importing nation and at the same time not affect the free world market.

In fairness to other free nations, the United States has so governed its program as not unduly to disrupt world markets.

But this does not mean that the United States intends to sit back and wait until other countries of the world have disposed of their production before we enter the selling field. In other words, the United States intends to go all out for a rugged selling program and give its competitors a good fight for available markets.

FEEDING THE WORLD BETTER [7]

The Government does not at this time have "$7 billion worth of food wasting in Government storage bins." The total commitments of the Commodity Credit Corporation do total around $7 billion, but this includes both the commodities owned by the Government and loans on commodities under Government price support. . . .

There is a question, of course, as to just what is surplus, and we do have need for a carryover of grain and other commodities from season to season. In fact, the farm act of 1954 established certain set-asides or carryovers which are not to be counted as surplus in arriving at the level of price supports. This was one suggestion by President Eisenhower. It is true, however, that in the case of wheat and dairy products our surpluses are top-heavy. In the case of feed grains, drought has on one or two occasions cut the crop production to a point where the corn in storage proved a boon.

There are other ways in which so-called surpluses can be turned into a blessing rather than a curse.

The United States has been selling some of the surplus, and to date a total of $453 million worth of surplus commodities has been sold to foreign countries in their local currencies—these sales are to be over and above normal purchase by such countries. These sales have been under the provisions of Public Law 480 and around $250 million worth had been sold in the last fiscal year. In many instances these sales for local currencies make

[7] From "Surpluses", a letter to the editors of *Christian Century*, by J. Stuart Russell, farm editor, Des Moines *Register & Tribune*. *Christian Century*. 72:338. March 16, 1955. Reprinted by permission.

possible the leaving of funds within the country for economic development or technical assistance programs.

But there is still another type of distribution in which church people should be interested. They are familiar with the food parcels to Berlin, the aid to the people in the Danube area —on both sides of the Iron Curtain—where crops were short this year, and the making of food available to relieve hunger in areas where food supplies have been short in recent years—Yugoslavia, India and Pakistan.

In the last half of 1954 a total of 442 million pounds of food was donated at home and abroad. These donations consisted largely of butter, cheese, dried milk, beef and gravy, dry beans and shortening. The supplies went to schools, institutions and needy persons in this country, while about 45 per cent of the total went for foreign distribution. Some of these donations were made direct to the countries for distribution to needy people, while Church World Service, CARE, the United Nations Children's Fund and War Relief Services, the American Friends Service Committee and others participated in the distribution of the donated food. In some cases, school lunch programs have been aided by such donations. In addition to all this, the United States within the last six months has bartered $93 million worth of surplus commodities for strategic materials.

All this barter, donation, and sale for local foreign currencies may not add up to a very big percentage of the total, but I think you will see that hungry people are benefiting from the fact that we have more on hand than we can consume here. On the basis of my own observation in most of the countries in Asia and the Far East, I am convinced that judiciously placed donations can help relieve hunger—and distrust and suspicion which some of the Asian countries now have of the United States, and trade with those nations can help them to a higher standard of living. Trade with these nations enables them to maintain their self-respect and dignity. This is much better than dumping our surpluses in such a way that the economy of any other nation might be injured.

PROBLEMS OF SELLING ABROAD [8]

An important reason for hoping that we can sell our surpluses abroad is that overseas needs during the war helped stimulate agricultural expansion over here. . . .

Agricultural production is quite elastic when it comes to expanding, at least as long as we have slack in our productive capacity which can be taken up. . . .

Unfortunately, the export market for farm products is not unlimited. This is a point which many Americans appear to miss. As already indicated, exports of such products as wheat and cheese have tapered off considerably with agricultural restoration in Western Europe and with enlarged supplies from other exporters seeking a market. Moreover, while dollars are not as short in supply as they were during the war and early postwar years, the "dollar shortage" still plays a part. . . .

The fact that the British customers may have sufficient pounds or the French buyers may have francs does not enable them to buy our products unless their money can be converted into dollars. Trade today is hampered decidedly by lack of convertibility. . . .

International trade is an exchange of goods and services. Exports pay for imports and vice versa. . . . This point is missed by those who in the same breath clamor for more restrictions on imports and more selling abroad. A country which insists upon curbing its imports must be willing to kiss some of its export market goodbye. Sales on credit and foreign investments affect the timing of settlements but do not alter the basic idea, that payment eventually must be in goods and services. . . .

Commodity Credit Corporation holdings . . . have accumulated because markets have not stood ready to absorb all of the available supplies at the prices at which they have been held. That is a logical result of any effort to maintain prices at levels above those which the markets would otherwise establish. . . .

[8] From "American Agriculture and Foreign Economic Policy," by O. B. Jesness, head, Department of Agricultural Economics, University of Minnesota. In *United States Agriculture: Perspectives and Prospects*; background papers and final report of Seventh American Assembly, Harriman, New York, May 5-8, 1955. The Assembly. Columbia University. New York 27. p79-88. Reprinted by permission.

Such prices become attractive to other countries. They are magnets which draw supplies to our markets. Here we have one source of conflict between our price support programs and international trade.

A not unnatural reaction to such imports is to say "Of course, we can't be Atlas and support the market for the whole world." What appears to be an easy way out is to bar these imports by outright embargoes or to limit their volume by the use of imports quotas. The threat of interference from imports was recognized early in the farm program. Congress added Section 22 to the Agricultural Adjustment Act in 1935 to provide specific authority to restrict imports which interfere with price support programs. . . .

Some other nations find it hard to reconcile our action on this front with our urgings on other countries to "earn" the dollars they need to buy from us, to lower their trade barriers, and to expand their international trade. In international trade conferences, representatives of the United States discover that our actions do not improve their bargaining position. . . .

Price supports create some problems on the export side as well. Exports have appeared as a promising solution to burdensome stocks. Pressure is brought to move these supplies. The law restricts the sale of stored products in domestic markets. Such disposals cannot undercut or interfere with the market. Sales at lower prices for export, however, are authorized.

It is easy for us to think of the rest of the world as being hungry for our surpluses and, therefore, of their being eager buyers. We tend to forget that we are not the only supplier. European nations which are among our best customers are also important food producers in their own right. . . .

Some form of two-price operation often is advocated to expand exports. This involves selling for export at lower prices than those maintained at home. . . . Our exports under the international Wheat Agreement are in this category. We use subsidy payments to move out some fruits and other products. We have offered butter for sale in export at a price well below domestic levels. Hence, some use of such a scheme is possible in certain situations. Does this justify the hope that it can be expanded to the point where it will remove surpluses, or at least make a real dent in our stocks? To help us get some answer to that question we need to examine limitations as well as possibilities.

"Export dumping" is one of these limitations. . . . Some contend that dumping is not involved unless products are sold abroad at prices below those prevailing in the *world* market. That is not the way dumping is defined. Export dumping refers to selling for export at lower prices than those prevailing in the *domestic* market of the selling country. . . .

The trouble comes when the dumped products compete with home production. Our producers may see unfair competition in such sales and demand protection against them. Producers in other countries may see our efforts to dump farm surpluses in the same light.

Besides, other exporters may look at our dumping operations with something less than enthusiasm. New Zealand and Denmark cannot be expected to sit back complacently and watch us make inroads on their markets by dumping our stocks of dairy products. Canada has a lot of wheat for which it wants a market and self-interest compels that country to keep an eye on how our operations affect its sales prospects. . . .

Whether we realize it or not, we are trying to get a larger slice of the market by taking it away from someone else.

We need to note also an additional consequence of export dumping. Where the object is to get rid of surpluses, we can't sit idly by and see the dumped products returning to our markets. . . . This applies not only to the products themselves but to goods made from them. For instance, if we sell cotton to foreign mills at prices below those charged our own textile mills, are the latter expected to offer no protest against the finished goods which flow to our markets as a result? . . .

Will international commodity agreements solve the export problem? The International Wheat Agreement is an illustration of an arrangement of this type. . . . Briefly, this agreement provides for the division of the wheat it covers into specific quotas. . . . Each exporting nation agrees to supply its quota at the maximum price in response to demands from importing nations, and each importer is obligated to take its quota at the minimum price. That is, the exporters are assured the minimum price for their quotas, and the importers are assured a supply equal to their quotas at the maximum price. Typically, sales have been at prices in between these extremes. This may not continue if available surpluses increase.

If domestic prices are maintained at levels above those at which sales are made within the agreement, the exporting nation must pay its producers the difference. Sales of the United States have required the Treasury to make up the difference. The anti-dumping restrictions are avoided because the importing nations are parties to the agreement.

The International Wheat Agreement has been criticized by some as being a form of cartel. It does take on some features of a cartel in that it allocates the market and establishes minimum and maximum prices. Others call attention to the fact that the participation of importing nations protects their interests as buyers, a situation not customarily found in cartels.

Another criticism of such agreements is that they encourage "state" trading because of the prominent part played by governments in making and carrying them out. . . . It may be in order to note in this connection that export and domestic trading are not separate and distinct. Instead, they are different facets of the same thing—the market. If governments expand their direct participation in foreign markets, they may find it difficult to refrain from extending their activities in the domestic market as well. . . .

The possibilities of international agreements in expanding and improving international trade deserve full exploration. However, it would be a mistake to view them as automatic solvents to surpluses. Expanding exports still depend on finding buyers in other countries for the goods we have to sell.

But what about disposal abroad through other than usual market channels? Two types of operations will be reviewed briefly. One is that of accepting local currencies in lieu of dollars for the products sold. The other is that of outright gifts. Congress has authorized expenditures of up to $1 billion over a three-year period for these purposes. Of this, $300 million are available for financing gifts of surplus products.

Acceptance of payment in local currencies is intended to overcome the lack of dollar exchange. The receiving country still has to pay, but does so in its own money rather than in ours. Consequently, it does not have to offset such purchases by exports to provide means of payment. But if such sales are to expand our exports, they must be in addition to, rather than merely the replacement of, other sales. . . .

A problem which such sales create is the use to be made of the local currencies which we take in exchange. If it so happens that we have acquired or intend to acquire and develop military bases in the receiving countries, the funds may be applied to that purpose. At times it may be possible to use them to buy strategic supplies wanted by us for stock piling. In such a situation it may be possible to barter some surplus products for the strategic material without resort to local currencies. . . .

We can treat these funds as we have counterpart funds in connection with other postwar aids. That is, we can turn the funds back to the purchasing country for its use in ways acceptable to us. Such operations fail to yield direct repayment. In fact, they become gifts. We must appraise the burden they impose on American taxpayers.

Local currencies might be used to buy goods to be brought to the United States. This will expand trade, providing it avoids replacement of other trading. Such an operation would almost certainly raise all sorts of complaints over government competition with private trading and domestic production.

Selling for local currencies does not promise unlimited possibilities, although it should be explored as one of the avenues for expanding trade and developing markets. . . .

There is still another way of disposing of surpluses, namely by giving them away to other countries. This gets away from the knotty problems of foreign exchange and dollar shortage because payment comes from the Americans. . . .

If the operation is to yield net results in reducing stocks, the gifts must not replace sales. Such gifts do not increase the total disposal but merely reduce returns. If our gifts replace the sales of other exporting nations, we will soon hear about it. In fact, we already have had reactions of this kind. . . .

In our efforts to donate sizable amounts to relieve want elsewhere, another problem we encounter is that we do not have available adequate machinery in those countries to make sure the products will go to the right places. It is not always simple to avoid having some of the gifts diverted to selfish ends by "sticky fingers" in between.

Moreover, there are indications that there is something less than complete enthusiasm in receiving countries over a temporary or "one-shot" deal. We may pat ourselves on the back in praise of our own generosity. However, other countries may regard our action as being one created by a desire to get rid of burdensome stocks. They may point out that, if we really are serious in providing help, we will do so on a continuing basis— even to the point of self denial if supplies become short. . . .

We may win friends for our side by means of our surpluses. We may also create opposition. It is a program which must be operated with good judgment. At best, disposal through these channels is likely to be of modest proportions in comparison with the stocks we have on hand. It does not promise to solve continued overproduction.

V. ACREAGE "RETIREMENT" PROGRAMS

EDITOR'S INTRODUCTION

The Administration's proposal for a "soil bank," including an "acreage reserve" and a "conservation reserve," is discussed in this section, along with alternative land "retirement" proposals by farmers' and other groups.

Secretary of Agriculture Benson, in the first article, presents the Administration's program, as substantially embodied in the Agricultural Act of 1956. A national news magazine discusses the operation of this program. Another magazine suggests that its effect may be to keep in agriculture marginal operators who would do better in other occupations.

Three succeeding articles give the concepts of two leading farmers' organizations and of a conservation group which fathered the concept of acreage "retirement." These selections discuss the objectives and operation of acreage "retirement" plans.

An agricultural economist discusses conservation measures in general and their use to bolster farm prices and income. A final article tells of a farmer's legal resistance to restrictions in the Government's acreage-control programs.

THE ADMINISTRATION'S PROGRAM [1]

To help bring about a balance of supplies and markets, the President proposed the establishment of a soil bank, which would be in two parts.

One part . . . would be called the acreage reserve. This is really a deferred-production plan. It would be voluntary and temporary, aimed at reducing production, and hence carryover, of those crops which today are in greatest surplus. The President recommended that the Congress consider this plan for wheat, cot-

[1] From statement by Secretary of Agriculture Ezra Taft Benson before the Senate Committee on Agriculture and Forestry, 84th Congress, 2d session, January 12, 1956. Department of Agriculture. Washington 25, D.C. January 1956. p 1-30.

ton, corn and rice. He set up as a target the reduction of carry-over for these crops to normal in three or four years.

Essence of the program is that farmers would voluntarily reduce production below their allotted acres. They would place specific acres into the reserve, receiving in return, as compensation, certificates which would be redeemable by the Commodity Credit Corporation in cash or in kind. Basis for the value of the certificates would be the normal yield on the designated reserve acres.

With production reduced, commodities now in government hands could be used to supply market needs. Thus CCC stocks could be reduced without depressing current market prices.

Farm income would be protected and increased during this adjustment.

As we have considered the acreage reserve program, certain principles have emerged which seem essential to its success.

1. The inducement offered farmers would have to be generous. Before farmers would comply they would have to feel that their net income would be at least as high as if they planted their allotted acres. Broad participation is necessary to assure success of the program. In establishing the percentage of the normal yields on the reserve acres which would determine the value of the certificates, we will have to take account of the farmer's alternatives, since that is what the farmers themselves will do. Legislation should establish suitable criteria and leave room for administrative discretion.

2. The acreage reserve program will work only for allotment crops. [i.e., crops limited by acreage restrictions or marketing agreements—Ed.]. Sale of stocks back into the market would be disastrous unless room is created in the market by a cutback in current production. Without such cutbacks, prices would be forced down. Or, if price support is provided, other stocks would move into CCC hands to offset the stocks moved out.

The program must be so operated as to give a lift to the market, not to beat down prices.

3. The acreage reserve program is not a substitute for a vigorous disposal policy.

CCC should continue and strengthen its efforts to sell or otherwise dispose of its commodities abroad and at home. Failing this, we might fail to reduce our stocks and the objective of the program would be lost.

An aspect of this program is common to all programs which rely on acreage limitations in order to hold production in check. Farmers may intensify operations, increase yields and partially offset the effect of the program. However, the size of the acreage cut proposed and the temporary nature of the program seem to me to give good reason for anticipating success.

The scope of the acreage reserve program could be impressive. If applied to wheat, cotton, corn and rice it could create a place in the market for more than a billion dollars' worth of Commodity Credit Corporation stocks in a year's time.

We would use the surplus to use up the surplus.

An increase in net income of farmers would come from buoyancy in the price structure caused by evidence to the trade that the surplus problem was finally coming under control. . . .

Income from the certificates would more than replace net income from sales of products from the reserve acres. The very fact that farmers would come into the program would itself indicate that they considered this their better alternative.

The program would have an insurance feature in this respect: even though crops might fail, the cooperating farmer would still receive a certificate based on normal yields from the reserve acres, which would have a cash value.

The acreage reserve program would be largely and perhaps wholly financed by commodities already owned by the Government rather than by a new outlay of funds.

In terms of alternatives the acreage reserve program is not costly, but economical. Whether we shall be able to avoid a loss by taking any other course is doubtful indeed. Storage costs run about $1 million a day. In about eight years, the carrying costs on a bushel of wheat equal the value of the wheat. Time and shrinkage, storage and other costs are eroding away the present value of these stocks. Consequently, the real cost to the Government—taking these and other facts into consideration—will be substantially less than the apparent cost in payments made on certificates.

Above all there is the price-depressing effect of the surplus, which levies a heavy and growing burden on our farm and ranch people. Our economists estimate that the huge surpluses reduced farm income in 1955 by the staggering sum of more than $2 billion. This is nearly 20 per cent of net farm income. No apologies are required for the cost of a program which gives real hope for removing so heavy a burden.

There is no plan which can solve quickly problems which have been many years in developing. We must be careful not to overpromise. But the soil bank, with the acreage reserve program and with the conservation reserve, which I am about to describe, will make sizable contribution toward a vital balancing of supplies with market demands.

The second part of the soil bank proposed by the President is a long-range program called the conservation reserve. This, too, would be voluntary. It would be open to all farmers regardless of the crops they grow. Objective would be to shift 25 million acres from cropland to forage, trees, or water storage. This shift would be intended as a long-range adjustment in land use. Some of our less productive lands would be brought into the program, as well as some of the acres which have been diverted out of wheat and cotton into feed grains and other crops.

Government would bear a fair share of the costs involved in establishing suitable cover. . . . Further, as the farmer reorganizes his farm along these soil conserving lines, the Government would provide certain annual payments for a period of years related to the length of time needed to establish the new use of the land. Since this annual payment on the conservation reserve would be forthcoming regardless of yields, this program as well as the acreage reserve program has an element of crop insurance.

On both the acreage reserve and the conservation reserve, historic acreage allotments would be protected. There would be no grazing on the acreage reserve. Grazing would be prohibited on the conservation reserve for a specified period following the establishment of cover, and in no case would grazing be permitted if the stand of grass would thereby be endangered.

The acres set aside under this provision should be specific acres so as to remove them from the rotation.

In recommending this program, the President thus emphasized its advantages in conserving and improving our soil, water and forest resources:

> We cannot accurately predict our country's food needs in the years ahead, except that they will steadily increase. We do know, however, that the sound course both for today and tomorrow is wisely to safeguard our precious heritage of food-producing resources so we may hand on an enriched legacy to future generations. The conservation reserve program will contribute materially to that end. . . .

If to the proposals in the President's message we add the Watershed Act and the Water Facilities Act of 1954, and add still further the incentives for conservation offered in the Internal Revenue Code of 1954, we then have the most extensive program of all time for the improvement and protection of our natural resources. . . .

I should like to make clear the meaning of the soil bank to livestock farmers. Our excessive supplies of feed grain have unduly stimulated the production of hogs and the feeding of cattle, with resulting low prices for both. The soil bank will cut into the production of feed grains, including corn if the acreage reserve program can be adapted to that crop. This would tend to shorten the supply of feed grain, lift the feed grain price structure and reduce the present incentive for excessive production of grain-consuming livestock. The effect would be to bolster prices, especially of hogs and fed cattle.

WHAT'S THIS SOIL BANK IDEA? [2]

The soil bank idea . . . is to have the Government rent part of each farm and retire the rented acres from production—put them in a soil bank. These idle acres could not be used, even for pasturing livestock or making hay. Amount of rental payments to farmers could reach $1 billion a year or more. . . .

[2] From an article in *U.S. News & World Report*. 39:30-1. November 11, 1955. Reprinted from *U.S. News & World Report*, an independent weekly news magazine published at Washington. Copyright 1955 United States News Publishing Corporation.

Before present control programs went into effect, the operator of a typical farm planted, on the average, about 100 acres of corn, 30 acres of wheat. His total of 220 acres was rounded out with other crops.

Under the present program to curb surpluses, the farmer must cut his corn acreage by about one sixth and his wheat acreage by about one third. This means taking 16 acres out of corn and 10 acres out of wheat, a total of 26 acres.

But the farmer, like any manufacturer, doesn't want to let part of his plant be idle. So he shifts the 26 acres taken out of wheat and corn into crops on which there are no acreage curbs. As a result, surpluses are building up in virtually every crop that farmers produce.

The soil bank proposal enters at this point. The plan, according to its advocates, would halt the build-up of surpluses by keeping the acres diverted from wheat and corn completely out of production.

These diverted, "surplus" acres would be planted to grasses and soil-building plants, such as clover and alfalfa. Fertility would be "banked" in the soil. Present soil-conservation payments would help pay the cost of planting this soil bank. The bank would be fenced off, literally, from the rest of the farm so that no livestock could graze on it. Even if the farmer were short of feed, he could not go onto these idle acres to cut hay.

In return for establishing this soil bank, the farmer would get a payment of so much an acre, direct from the Government. This would prevent his income from dropping as a result of the cutback in production caused by keeping the diverted acres idle.

Farm income would be bolstered further, say those who are pushing the plan, by the fact that price-depressing surpluses would be cut down, thus boosting prices in farm markets.

The idea's appeal to urban voters is based on the banking of fertility in the soil where it would be available in future years to meet emergencies, such as war or drought, or the needs of a rapidly expanding population. Nonfarm people, it is held, would consider this sounder than the present program under which billions of Government dollars are tied up in surplus farm commodities stored up in bins and warehouses.

Midwestern farm politicians see in the soil bank plan three big advantages: a shot in the arm for farm income; a way to reduce the hoard of surplus farm products; an appeal to urban voters. . . .

Estimates of the cost to taxpayers range from $200 million to $1.5 billion annually. Some versions of the plan would pay the farmer a percentage of the appraised value of the land taken out of production. Others would pay only interest and taxes on the idle acres. Still others would reimburse the farmer on the basis of the average production of the land. . . .

[Critics of the plan] say that its ability to curb surpluses has been oversold. They maintain that farmers will produce about as much on fewer acres, by retiring their poor land to the soil bank and giving their good land more attention and fertilizer.

These critics say the soil bank idea is nothing more than a refinement of a New Deal farm plan of the 1936-38 period, under which farmers were paid by the Government to put land into soil-conservation crops. During that period, crop-production figures show, supplies of wheat and cotton increased.

Advocates of today's soil bank plan say, however, that it has been improved in that the acres taken out of production must be kept completely idle. The president of the Iowa Farm Bureau Federation concedes that farmers would step up production per acre. However, in his opinion, if 20 per cent of the nation's crop land were put into the soil bank, there would be a 10 per cent cutback in farm production over a three-year period. This, he feels, would give the Government time to get the surplus stockpile down to manageable size.

The plan also is attacked on the ground that it would be hard to police. "Who is going to go up and down farm roads to make sure that cattle don't break through fences and eat grass off the soil bank acres?" asks one critic.

Another point of disagreement is over just how much the plan will do to firm up sagging farm income. Farm expenses, such as taxes, interest and machinery costs will go on, say the critics, even though part of the farmer's land is idle. And, if there is no reduction in surpluses, income will not be bolstered by higher farm prices.

WILL PLAN HELP THOSE WHO SHOULD BE HELPED? [3]

The Administration has . . . decided that a system of flexible supports is not enough to satisfy the farmer, or to solve what the President calls "the paradox facing our farm families," namely a decline in farm prices and incomes in the midst of a great industrial boom. . . .

He proposes . . . making a direct attack on farm surpluses through a new gimmick, the "soil bank." Under an immediate "acreage reserve" plan the Government will pay farmers who voluntarily reduce their plantings in certain crops, notably wheat and cotton, and possibly corn and rice, below present allotments. Under a long-range "conservation reserve" scheme, furthermore, the Government would pay farmers who take land out of any kind of cultivation and turn it back to forage, timber and other uses. All told, the plan aims to take some 40 million acres out of production at a cost to the taxpayer of about $1 billion per year. And initially, at least, until surpluses are reduced, this would be piled on top of the $1.3 billion now going out for farm benefits.

All this is a very considerable increase in the subsidization of American agriculture, especially for an Administration that prides itself on Government economy. What is troublesome, however, is not just the cost of the program but its assumption that the Government owes any class in this country a predetermined standard of living and income. It is troublesome, too, that while the President has clearly defined part of the farm problem—namely, the existence of surpluses—he has by no means faced up to the whole of it. He believes there are too many acres in production in the United States to yield a satisfactory balance between supply and demand for farm commodities, but, after all, the acres are in cultivation because farmers are there to cultivate them. And a program whose major political appeal is to drive up farm prices and incomes (by paying farmers to produce nothing) may well serve to keep some farmers on the

[3] From " 'Farm Problem': 1956 Edition." *Fortune.* 53:85-6. February 1956. Reprinted by special permission of the editors. Copyright 1956, Time Inc.

land indefinitely who might otherwise seek more rewarding occupations, to their own and the economy's benefit.

At the least, any sensible Government policy must take account of certain controlling facts that powerfully influence the farmer's position. The first fact is that the demand for food products by their very nature is not apt to rise as fast as demand for many other products. The second fact is that, owing to research (in part sponsored by Government) and increasing capital investment, productivity has been advancing on the farm even faster than in industry. As a result, fewer and fewer farmers are required to meet the needs of the country, and farm population, 25 per cent of the total population in 1930, is now down to 13 per cent. In the next quarter-century, on some estimates, it could fall from roughly 22 million to 17 million; farm output, however, will rise substantially.

These developments may be unwelcome to those who conceive of the farmer as a part of a fixed and immutable class, but they help explain why the farmer today is far better off than most politicians, and indeed the President, seem to think. Between 1947 and 1955 total farm net income as well as prices did decline; but in the same period some 2 million people moved off the land, and those who stayed found many supplementary means of income. As a result farm income per capita, which was $788 in 1947, is estimated at $856 for 1955.

Moreover, these average figures for farm population tell only part of the story. As technologies have advanced, farming has become a big business for those who succeed. In 1954 there were some 4.8 million farms in the United States. Of these, some 2 million, or 44 per cent of the total, probably produced over 90 per cent of the total of farm cash sales. These larger and more efficient farms are not in trouble today, and they account for the bulk of total farm assets, which have reached the tremendous figure of $162 billion. The real farm problem is centered on about 1 million farms that generate practically no cash income, and afford at best a subsistence living.

It is difficult to see how the President's new plan will aid these marginal farmers and, indeed, it could even do harm. In the first instance the bulk of soil bank subsidies is likely to go to the larger and more prosperous operators—a defect, also, of price-support payments. Faced with a choice of trying to reduce the acreage of a farm of twenty acres, or one with one thousand, Government officials (who will enjoy tremendous discretion in this matter) will probably find it easier to deal with the bigger unit. In this case the cash benefits will go to those who do not need them.

But even if it is assumed that some of the subsidy will "trickle down" to the little fellow, it is far from clear that this will really help him. On the contrary, Government checks for retiring some of his land will give him precisely the cash income that he needs to hang on in a precarious and fundamentally unsound situation. Certainly, if the President's aim is to help the man who needs the help, the taxpayer's money might be better spent on a clear-cut program for education and training for other jobs.

Defenders of the soil bank will, of course, argue that its main purpose is to get rid of present surpluses, and that if these are reduced, all farmers, great and small, will gain. Even here, however, large questions arise. As general acreage is taken out of production, all farmers will intensify their efforts to produce more on the land left in cultivation. Their ability to do so has been proved time and again. As the President somewhat ruefully admits, acreage allotments in 1955 were supposed to reduce the cotton crop to 10 million bales; actually nearly 15 million bales were forthcoming. What this means is that if the soil bank scheme is to work at all, Government regulations and controls must be tightened up and even extended. The Government, for instance, must be sure that land taken out of production is not used for grazing, lest this increase cattle raising and depress beef prices. As the whole history of price support proves, controlling production is exceedingly difficult short of collectivizing American agriculture completely. . . .

While the soil bank plan may have certain virtues, and certainly is preferable to a return to high and rigid price supports, it is no substitute for letting farm prices gradually find their own level and exert their normal influence in adjusting supply to demand.

On the record to date, it has been in those areas of agriculture . . . where the Government has interfered most, in wheat, in cotton, in peanuts, that the farmer has got himself into deeper and deeper trouble, and deeper and deeper obligations to the state. If the United States wishes to preserve agriculture as a way of life it cannot go on insulating it from the market forces and choices that guide other American citizens.

VIEWS OF THE GRANGE [4]

The Grange has long recognized and repeatedly stated that a form of land rental type program—preferably as closely related as we can honestly relate it to a long-range, sound soil conservation objective—has a real place in both emergency type farm legislation and in long-term permanent legislation. . . .

The acreage reserve program seems basically sound and substantially in accord . . . with Grange program and policy . . . insofar as Government-held stocks are concerned. . . .

We would warn against an erroneous assumption that a long-term operation of such an acreage reserve program will do anything constructively and progressively either to raise farm income or to make increasing contribution to the total national welfare. This acreage reserve program approach, in our judgment, has major potential value during either a one- or at most a two-year operation. The longer such a program is permitted to operate or the greater the length of time on which we may be willing to rely on such a program, the less value it will have.

We would, therefore, urge this Committee to think in terms of adequate incentive to make the acreage reserve program capable of doing two fundamental things and doing them to the greatest extent possible and practicable within one year's time. Those two things are:

(1) To "buy" a substantial adjustment between currently available markets and current agricultural supply; and

[4] From statement of Herschel D. Newsom, master, National Grange, at hearings of Senate Committee on Agriculture and Forestry. In *Price Support Program*; hearings, October 23, 1955-January 23, 1956. 84th Congress, 2nd Session. Superintendent of Documents. Washington 25, D.C. 1956. p3251-3.

(2) put dollars of purchasing power into the hands of the rural families of America—which we believe is highly desirable in the face of the situations that now confront us. . . .

We would especially urge that participation in this acreage reserve program must be a strictly voluntary determination on the part of the farmer himself. . . .

We firmly believe that the conservation reserve program . . . is basically sound and highly desirable. . . .

For the record, however, we would like to record Grange hope that the administration of this section of the act would take due account of the extensive network of soil-conservation districts across the nation. These soil-conservation districts can be of substantial value in making this kind of legislation really productive of long-term results, both to American farmers and to society as a whole.

VIEWS OF AMERICAN FARM BUREAU FEDERATION [5]

We favor the principle that in order to qualify for price supports, producers be required to put an acreage of soil-depleting cropland in the soil bank. . . . Producers receiving price supports should not be given Government benefits and at the same time be permitted to shift the acreage taken out of price-supported crops into the production of other crops. . . . [This] . . . constitutes unfair subsidization of competition with the producers of all other agricultural commodities.

The prohibition against the use of any retired land for the production of agricultural commodities or products, including livestock products, is a vital requirement of any program to withhold acreage from production. . . .

It is undesirable to limit or graduate the amount of price support which an individual producer may earn by reason of the size of a farm or ranch. [This] . . . would penalize efficiency, place a ceiling on opportunity, encourage the artificial

[5] From statement filed by American Farm Bureau Federation at hearings of Senate Committee on Agriculture and Forestry. In *Price Support Program*; hearings, October 23, 1955-January 23, 1956. 84th Congress, 2d session. Superintendent of Documents. Washington 25, D.C. 1956. p3515-16.

division of farms and ranches, and finally, result in increasing the cost of food and fiber to consumers by forcing the division of farms and ranches into uneconomic producing units. . . .

Any soil bank plan should have the objectives of helping to balance agricultural production with effective market demand, emphasizing conservation, contributing to a solution of the diverted acreage problem, facilitating a substantial reduction in the Government's inventories of surplus commodities, emphasizing the voluntary approach, protecting the rights of tenants on an equitable basis, including enough incentive to achieve a high percentage of participation, but using payments only to further the achievement of these objectives and not as an end in themselves.

Since accumulated surpluses are acting as a ceiling on farm prices and depressing farm income, we believe that a soil bank plan at this time should use the surplus stocks of Commodity Credit Corporation to reward the producers for placing acreage in the soil bank. We favor the "payment-in-kind" approach, since we do not believe that the soil bank plan should be kept in operation indefinitely and as the Commodity Credit Corporation stocks are liquidated, the program likewise could be terminated. We believe it would be possible to have a highly satisfactory soil bank plan if only a very nominal amount of newly appropriated funds were made available for that purpose, since the quantity of surplus stocks held by CCC are quite ample to make payments at this time. . . .

Apportionment among states, counties, and farms of acreages to be put in the bank is an unnecessary administrative burden which should be avoided.

Any soil bank payment should also be varied in such a manner as to fairly compensate producers for their real contribution to a reduction in production. This would necessitate being careful about making payments for merely withholding acreage from production for only one year. Arid areas, by holding acreage out of production merely one year, could build up a water supply on such land so that production the second year would be much greater than it would have been otherwise. Comparable situations would occur in humid areas for acreage only held out of production one year. . . .

Amendments to the marketing quota and acreage allotment provisions . . . should not be made in such a manner as to relieve individual producers from making a just contribution to the balancing of supplies with demand. The indefinite crediting of producers as having planted their allotment by the release and reapportionment of acres could have such effect. We are for the release and reapportionment of acreage allotments as they are presently established in the law. However, any acreage under-planted to qualify for payment under the surplus reduction and soil bank act should not be available for release and reapportionment to any other producer.

[Provisions of the Agricultural Act of 1956 follow the recommendations of the American Farm Bureau Federation much more closely than those of the Soil-Bank Association, described in the following article.—Ed.]

VIEWS OF SOIL-BANK ASSOCIATION [6]

The soil bank plan as proposed by the Soil-Bank Association would:

1. Establish a minimum base for hay, pasture, and soil-building crops for the various agricultural regions. [The Agricultural Act of 1956 did not establish such bases.—Ed.]

2. Offer incentive payments for soil-building acres in excess of this minimum base. [The 1956 Act provides payments in cash or in kind.—Ed.]

3. Establish the soil-building base for an individual farm in relation to soil class, and it would not be tied to an individual farmer's historical acreage. [The 1956 Act leaves this to each farmer.—Ed.]

[6] From statement by Melvin F. Gehlbach, chairman, board of directors, Soil-Bank Association, Lincoln, Illinois, at hearings of Senate Committee on Agriculture and Forestry. In *Price Support Program*; hearings, October 23, 1955-January 23, 1956. 84th Congress, 2d session. Superintendent of Documents. Washington 25, D.C. 1956. p3733-8.

4. Give all individual farms on comparable land classes a comparable proportionate base and give opportunity to earn soil bank incentive payments for an additional acreage of soil building. [The 1956 Act has no such provision.—Ed.]

The thing that bothers us tremendously is as folks are testifying in regard to the acreage reserve they seem to have in mind the high-yielding acre and shifting it out of production and think in terms they need a lot of money to shift that high-yielding acre.

Our approach is this: Let us shift the low-yielding acres on land that needs soil building into the soil bank plan. And we have lots of acres in this country . . . that with lower yields and lower fertility make no profit at all—and we plan that this incentive payment, if we can outweigh the low-yielding acres and those that are making losses instead of profits—if we can shift those into fertility building and really make a bold shift of that type of land we will protect net earnings for farmers and then build fertility on the proper acres. . . .

Feeder cattle profits, as well as net returns from beef cow herds, will have to be attractive before farmers will forgo their final fertility-reserve payment. The soil bank plan is designed for livestock farms as well as grain farms.

The increased acres of soil-building crops are more than a fertility reserve—they are a forage reserve on each and every farm. In case of drought or other emergency, this reserve can be brought into use if need outweighs incentive payment.

The decision to release much-needed feed to maintain cattle herds when drought, flood, or insect hazards strike, should be left with the farmer. The forage reserve is designed to meet the needs of the individual farm and have a degree of flexibility to protect farm income as well as a food supply for the nation.

How must we handle our Government-held surpluses? We believe we should:

1. Convert a portion of present farm surplus into a well-defined stockpile with provision for periodic replacement.

2. Adjust production below current needs to absorb the balance of the surplus into the market for use as soon as possible, not at half price but at full price. We are in accord with the

President's proposal to "recommend legislation to permit, under proper safeguards, sales at not less than support levels, plus carrying charges."

3. Instead of taking a substantial loss on the billions of dollars of agricultural commodities held by the Government, use a part of this money for an effective soil bank program to adjust production below current needs.

Nearly everyone agrees that it is cheaper to pay a farmer an incentive to expand soil-building acres than to overproduce cash crops and have to wonder what to do with it. In addition, the farmer receives extra earning in that he saves the cost of producing the surplus. . . .

A serious weakness of the acreage reserve program is that it does not reach the farms in noncompliance with allotments.

Lowering support prices and thus decreasing the differences between support price and market price only lessens the motivation force so that fewer farmers will comply with acreage allotments.

It may be difficult to obtain full voluntary compliance in the soil bank or any other plan in the near future. Farmers' participation would be determined largely by their attitude toward past programs as well as the present programs. As some farmers might find it advantageous not to cooperate, many farmers may wish to shift beyond their allotted soil-building acreage and receive the unused soil bank funds available from those who think it would be better to forgo payments and not adjust production.

In this way we may have only two thirds of the farmers participating but acrewise could attain effective compliance. Why not let those farmers who need it most adjust production and build fertility? Why not begin paying the farmers who cooperate, instead of penalizing them, as in the past?

In addition to the incentive payment inducing farmers to adjust production, we propose offering commodity loans at levels in relation to the compliance with soil bank acres. Farmers in full compliance should be eligible for full loan value. Farmers planting all cash crops and no soil-building crops would be eligible for only 50 per cent loan value. The farmer determines his own loan level by his degree of participation in production adjustment.

The proposed soil bank plan must be made effective beyond any normal program to protect price levels during the period of moving surplus stocks back into the market for consumption. An accelerated program to accomplish this would involve a vigorous approach for two or three years and then would be tempered, not ended, to keep agriculture in balance with the rest of the economy.

The money spent for incentive payments is not a direct subsidy or a dole. To receive this payment a farmer needs to forgo the income from cash crops making up our present surpluses and, instead, to build fertility to protect the food supply for the consumers of this nation and probably of the world. The cost of the program should be borne, not by farmers alone, but by all who benefit. . . .

Our soil bank plan would be applied as follows:

It can never be expected that all acreage eligible for payment will be shifted into soil building, but we can expect near 100 million acres of land now producing cash crops at a low yield per acre and returning little or no net profit per acre to come into the soil bank program.

When surpluses are reduced and production is brought into line with market needs the higher price will automatically shift land back into cash crops thus relieving the Government of providing the incentive payment. . . .

We would like to see soil bank payments made in two parts: A first payment to shift land use from grain to forage on the expected 100 million acres at an average payment of $8 per acre.

This payment would be related to the level of production of the various agricultural regions ranging from $3 to $15 per acre. There should be no restrictions on the use of forage for this first payment.

A second payment would be offered those farmers who forgo feeding the forage on these soil bank acres. This payment, too, would average around $8 per acre with a range similar to the first payment.

A good guess is that we would have at least 70 million acres of the 100 million acres affected by the second incentive payment to place into a fertility reserve the forage grown and not harvested or fed.

How much money will this program cost? If made effective it need not cost too much. Here are our estimates.

1st payment: 100 million acres, @ $8................. $800,000,000
2nd payment: 75 million acres (forage not fed), @ $8.... 600,000,000
————————
Total incentive (spending—not cost) $1,400,000,000

By adjusting production beyond current needs, enabling the Government to move the surplus into the market earlier, and thereby saving the cost of deterioration and storage, we should regain $600 million. This is based on a $6 billion storage holding, figuring a 10 per cent annual reduction in value.

CONSERVATION AS AN OBJECTIVE [7]

Conservation policy, like every other vital question of public policy, narrows down to a search for ways to reconcile conflicting interests. . . . First, there are inevitable conflicts between the goal of conservation and other objectives in the use of resources, and these conflicts can be resolved only by deliberate compromise. Second, the land use practices which are most profitable or least disadvantageous for the individual often will not coincide with the practices most conducive to conservation. Public action to make conservation feasible and desirable from the viewpoint of the private operator is the heart of public policy for the conservation of agricultural resources.

"Conservation" is a word of many meanings. We are safe in identifying it with "best use" of resources so long as we include *future* as well as *present* needs, and *social values* as well as *individual interests*. . . .

[7] From "Conservation of Agricultural Resources," by Raymond J. Penn, chairman, and C. W. Loomer, associate professor, Department of Agricultural Economics, University of Wisconsin. In *United States Agriculture: Perspectives and Prospects;* background papers and final report of Seventh American Assembly, Harriman, New York, May 5-8, 1955. The Assembly. Columbia University. New York 27. 1955. p 115-22. Reprinted by permission.

Conservation is only one of the many objectives of our farm policy. Among these other objectives, we seek to promote efficient production, stabilize farm prices, expand foreign markets, help farm tenants become owners, find new uses for farm products, help low-income farm families, improve rural community services, and many other things, most of which affect the use of land, indirectly at least. . . .

Farmers will not usually adopt a conservation practice until they know it is worth while. Unfortunately, conservation has become identified, to some extent, with postponement of income and with reduced current production. We commonly speak of "taking land out of production" to put it in grass or some other "conservation crop." Our farm programs have sometimes sought simultaneously to promote conservation and to reduce agricultural surpluses by encouraging shifts from soil-depleting crops to soil-conserving crops with less cash value. Actually, many recommended soil conservation practices increase yields, lower costs of production, and bring higher returns to the farmer. Terracing reduces erosion by retarding run-off and uses water more effectively for growing crops. Cultivation on the contour is said to take less tractor fuel than plowing in straight lines up and down the slopes. In other words, there is more and more reason to believe that the needs of soil conservation are met in large part by better farm management, with tillage practices, improved crop rotations, and fertility programs that are worth while from the standpoint of production and farm income alone.

In recent years, governmental conservation programs have emphasized the kinds of practices that will improve farm incomes in the immediate future as well as over the long years ahead. From the viewpoint of public policy, this is an important development because it gives added inducement for voluntary private action and suggests, moreover, that current public efforts to encourage farmers to conserve will not be as necessary after conservation practices once become established in the farming system. . . .

Every year but one in the past decade, the Federal Government has paid at least $200 million to American farmers for carrying out soil conservation practices on their own lands. These payments under the Agricultural Conservation Program illustrate how payments from the public treasury can be employed to further various objectives of conservation policy.

Conditional grants can induce farmers to embark on conservation enterprises they would be reluctant to undertake by themselves because of the economic risks involved. Conservation payments can cover a substantial part of the cost of changing over from current farming methods to a conservation plan, thus enabling farmers to make improvements they are unable to finance with their own resources. Either way, the new improvements may result in increased productivity and higher farm incomes that will permit farmers to carry on conservation practices, even though payments are subsequently reduced or eliminated.

Conservation payments may continue to be useful as partial support for practices that would never be entirely economic for an individual farm enterprise. As such, they represent the public's share of responsibility for the conservation measures needed to protect the national resources, especially in those cases where the social values of conservation are significantly different from private values. . . .

When the farmer tries to borrow money to finance a conservation project, he is likely to find that lending agencies have not worked out a policy covering such loans. As a result, he may find that he can borrow money only by paying high-risk rates of interest. Lack of credit on terms suited for conservation has proved to be a major deterrent.

Like any other businessman, the farmer has to keep a reserve of liquid assets to guard against emergencies. When he is faced with great uncertainties about the future of farm prices and farm income, he cannot afford to tie up his own assets in long-term investments in conservation. . . .

When a farm conservation plan, by improving the land, results in higher assessments and higher real-estate taxes, the investment looks less attractive. When the higher taxes must be paid year after year out of current income, while the farmer waits for deferred returns from his investment, conservation may prove uneconomic even in the long run.

The farmer who rents his farm often cannot afford to invest time and capital in soil improvements because he cannot be sure that he will remain on the farm long enough to benefit from his investment. On the other hand, the man who tries to become a farm owner by making a small down payment has little real security of tenure until he has time to build up his equity in the farm. The pressure of high fixed payments for taxes, interest, and debt retirement may force him to "mine" the soil in order to get the greatest immediate income.

Factors such as these which, strictly speaking, lie outside the scope of conservation policy in the usual sense, often prove to be critically important in the individual's decision to conserve— or not conserve—his resources. We noted earlier the need for a price system that would function to support and promote soil conservation. Perhaps equally important is the need for credit, taxation, and tenure institutions that will do the other tasks we want done and still provide adequate opportunity for a sound conservation program through voluntary private action.

A FARMER CHALLENGES CONTROLS [8]

An eighty-one-year-old chicken farmer . . . has asked the United States District Court of Philadelphia to declare unconstitutional the wheat price and acreage control features of the Federal farm and marketing administration acts, dating back to 1938. His arguments were reported in the *Wall Street Journal* of August 13, 1954:

In his suit against the United States Government, Joseph Blattner . . . asks that the Government be enjoined from preventing him from raising his usual crops on his own land, and from collecting a penalty from him . . .

The complaint charges that the Government is preparing to collect $179.20 from Mr. Blattner as a penalty for raising wheat in excess of Federally-stipulated allotments. A farmer since boyhood, he contends he

[8] From "Agrarian Reform," pamphlet by Paul L. Poirot, staff member, Foundation for Economic Education. The Foundation. Irvington-on-Hudson, N.Y. 1954. p 1-14. Reprinted by permission.

needs all the twenty-four acres of wheat he sowed this year to feed his six thousand laying hens, although the Government notified him he was alloted only sixteen acres and is penalizing him for the extra output. The action, the complaint states, takes Mr. Blattner's property without due process of law, thus depriving him of equal protection of the law while benefiting others without compensation to him, in violation of the Fifth Amendment to the Constitution. Mr. Blattner states he has never asked for nor received any assistance from Federal agencies.

The complaint adds that Mr. Blattner's chicken and egg output is sold within Montgomery County, Pennsylvania, involving no interstate trade, and that all corn and wheat he harvests goes to feed his own chickens. . . .

The complaint claims the acts of the Government will put Mr. Blattner out of business, since the prices of his eggs and chickens are not arbitrarily fixed, while the feed the Government "is forcing the plaintiff to buy to produce his product, is so fixed." . . .

Mr. Blattner . . . finds himself squeezed by the efforts of the Federal Government to hold prices of farm commodities at levels higher than the consumers are willing to pay. His complaint is that he is being taxed to help carry out a plan which is clearly injurious to him and to others with whom he is forcibly restrained from trading. . . .

In effect the plaintiff has been told that if he wants to feed more than a certain amount of wheat to his own chickens, he must purchase that additional amount from the Government at the Government's price. He may not raise the wheat on his own land by his own efforts, unless he pays a penalty. He may not buy the wheat from any other farmer unless that other farmer has adhered to all the Federal controls. In other words, the Government has granted itself a monopoly control of the wheat supply of the United States of America. It is illegal to deal in wheat except on terms prescribed by the monopolist. And as the plaintiff explains, such monopolistic controls are not confined to wheat. . . .

Any governmental tampering with prices must necessarily reduce the volume of trading. By definition, and in practice, the competitively determined free market price always allows the maximum of trade. At the free market price, and at no other price can there be a matching of supply and demand. A lower price may attract buyers but drives sellers from the market;

a higher price attracts sellers but drives the buyers away. This means, then, that governmental price controls should only apply to trading which is deemed undesirable, for the inevitable effect is to curb trade.

Apparently, at the moment, the unrestricted buying and selling of eggs is officially desirable, but not free market trade in wheat. . . .

If the plaintiff can produce eggs most economically by also growing some of the feed for his flock on his own land, why should he not be allowed to do so?

["The United States Circuit Court of Appeals for the Third District," Mr. Blattner's attorney writes, "affirmed the decision of the United States District Court for the Eastern District of Pennsylvania, which sustained the Government's position that the Act was constitutional and the Government had the right to fine Blattner for growing wheat on his own farm to feed his own chickens."—Ed.]

VI. FAMILY AND LOW-INCOME FARMS

EDITOR'S INTRODUCTION

Any solution of agriculture's problems must deal with the family farm and its place in American society and economy and with the marginal producer who barely manages to cling to his land.

Secretary of Agriculture Benson, in the first article in this section, calls attention to the situation of our rural "under-privileged" and outlines the Administration's proposals for broad assistance to this group. Many of these suggestions have been embodied in the Agricultural Act of 1956.

A business magazine suggests that larger shares for fewer farmers may be at least part of the answer and that marginal farmers might be better off economically in other occupations.

Finally, a farm magazine editor tells what must be done if that traditional American institution, the family farm, is to remain with us.

OUR RURAL "UNDERPRIVILEGED" [1]

In compliance with your request in your special congressional message on agriculture last year, I have given particular attention to the problems of farm people with low incomes. The report which accompanies this letter is addressed to that subject.

The problem is more basic than low incomes expressed in dollars; the fact that it embodies human values—the lives and welfare of people and of families—gives rise to the title of the report, "Development of Agriculture's Human Resources."

The report has been prepared by the Department of Agriculture with the cooperation of many organizations, groups and individuals both within and outside of Government. The study

[1] From "Government Program for Low-Income Farmers," a letter by Secretary of Agriculture Ezra T. Benson, transmitted by the President to the Congress in a message April 27, 1955. *Current History*. 28:368-71. June 1955. Reprinted by permission.

brings into bold relief the stubborn fact that large numbers of farm people with small farms have shared unequally in our country's economic and social progress.

Many of these people wish to increase their contribution to the nation's production of goods and services, and thereby improve their own levels of living. Helping them to accomplish this objective will not only improve the well-being of those directly concerned, but will also add to the nation's strength. Prudence as well as sympathy should impel us to strengthen our activity in this area.

Price support programs are of little help to most of these people. Production per farm is so low that only a few dollars can be added to incomes by price supports.

Problems of low income in agriculture, and efforts to alleviate these problems, are not of recent origin. Over the years, many effective methods have been developed for increasing the productivity and raising the incomes of these farm people. Among these methods are new educational techniques, supervised credit, vocational training, and the providing of employment information.

Much has been accomplished in this field during the past several years. Social Security was extended last year to more than five million farmers and farm workers. Research work has been increased. The farm unit approach, as an educational method, has been expanded and adapted to the social circumstances of farm people with low incomes. Opportunities for off-farm employment have been improved. Educational opportunities have been broadened. But these programs have not been fully coordinated, and operations have been on an insufficient scale.

The broad objectives of the report are clear—to help farm people with low gross incomes achieve the goals to which they themselves aspire.

The program recommended in the report is long-range in nature. Parts of the program are new; other parts have been operating, though not fully developed, for a number of years. Many other methods and operating procedures not reflected in the report will be generated as work progresses.

Clearly, a broad, aggressive, well-coordinated assault is urgently needed. New measures must be launched; established activities must be strengthened. To achieve maximum success, all elements of American life in rural areas must participate in the program. Civic and business leadership, farm organizations, schools, churches, community and service clubs, local, state and Federal governmental agencies, must all assist in a long sustained comprehensive attack on the problems of the low-income farm families.

After careful consideration of the problems and conclusions presented in the report, I recommend the launching of pilot operations in not less than fifty of the one thousand low-income counties during the coming fiscal year. In addition, community development programs can be undertaken. Thus practical experience can be gained in a limited number of areas, and those elements of the program which proved most successful can be utilized as the program is broadened. In the pilot operations, efforts will be made to develop the best practical program of action, having in mind the people, the resources, and the whole range of opportunities. Real progress can be made only through emphasis on matching local plans and efforts with both the individual needs and the actual resources available for individual improvement. The program would comprise the following elements, the proper balance among them to be determined by the special circumstances of each area:

1. Expand and adapt agricultural extension work to meet the needs of low-income farmers and part-time farmers.

2. Develop needed research in farm and home management, human nutrition, population, marketing, and in evaluating experience gained by the pilot program.

3. Provide additional credit for low-income farmers, and extend Farmers Home Administration services to part-time farmers.

4. Increase technical assistance, such as provided by the soil conservation service, to low-income farmers.

5. Request the Department of Health, Education and Welfare to encourage the states to expand vocational training in rural areas of low income, instituting as many as twelve pilot opera-

tions during the school term starting in the fall of 1955 in order to gain experience needed for broad expansion of this extremely vital part of the total program.

6. Request the Department of Labor to strengthen the employment service in rural areas and further to adapt it to the needs of rural people. Areas of rural underemployment should be identified and included as part of the labor market services to make occupational adjustments easier.

7. Undertake to get more effective programs developed to induce the expansion of industry in rural low-income areas, using facilities of the Departments of Labor and Commerce and the Office of Defense Mobilization.

8. Call upon the state agricultural colleges to make substantial research and extension contributions to a cooperative venture, employing in part the increased Federal funds already included in the 1956 budget request.

9. Aggressively encourage farm, business and other leadership to assume local responsibility and to unite in efforts to aid in the development of agriculture's human resources, using trade area and community development programs to increase incomes of farmers and raise living standards. Expansion of these "self-help" programs should be assisted by the various governmental agencies concerned.

Certain actions by the Congress will be needed in order that this program may be effectively launched:

10. Farmers Home Administration should be authorized to make loans to part-time farmers.

11. Legislation should be enacted which would concentrate special funds outside the present agricultural extension formula for the purpose of conducting pilot programs and extending assistance to low-income farmers.

12. Appropriation requests are being recommended for your consideration in addition to those in the regular budget for fiscal 1956, to initiate work proposed in this report involving extension, research, soil conservation, farm loans and related services.

13. Lending authority of about $30 million should be provided for the Farmers Home Administration. Draft legislation

and budget estimates relating to these recommendations have been prepared.

Certain administrative arrangements will also be required:

14. The Secretary of Agriculture should coordinate the administration of the total program. A principal official of the department should be designated to assume the direct administration of the program. Moreover, two coordinating committees will be needed:

a. An interdepartmental committee, and

b. A committee within the Department of Agriculture to coordinate the work of its participating agencies.

15. The Secretary of Agriculture should be required, in September of each year beginning 1956, to submit a comprehensive report to the President on the progress of activities directed toward alleviating the problems of low-income farmers and on plans for advancing the program, thus regularly focusing attention on the program and fixing responsibility for its administration.

The program outlined for the coming year must be expanded as experience is gained; the above recommendations are but a logical first step toward implementing the far broader program delineated in the report. The desirable rate of expansion and the emphasis to be given to various segments of the program in subsequent years will stand more clearly revealed as the program herein proposed evolves.

The accompanying report has been in preparation for more than a year. It draws on information supplied by farmers and by the major farm organizations. State agricultural experiment stations and other research institutions contributed substantially. The judgment and counsel of practically all recognized authorities in this field were made available. Organized labor, business and religious groups were consulted as well as agricultural groups.

Information and guidance were furnished by the Departments of Agriculture; Defense; Commerce; Health, Education and Welfare; Labor; the Farm Credit Administration, and the Veterans Administration. Congressional reports and publications were also of valuable assistance. Of special value was the experienced judgment of men in local communities, in state agencies, and in the Department of Agriculture who for many years have dealt at first hand with these problems.

The study was a cooperative undertaking. Task forces, heading up in the Department of Agriculture but with personnel from all the above-named agencies, prepared background material. The National Agricultural Advisory Commission provided facilities for review. Substantial agreement was reached by all participating groups on the recommendations contained in the report.

The report, which I herewith forward as a report of this department, is intended as a general guide and study document rather than as a blueprint. I am convinced that the report both reveals an awareness of the magnitude of the serious problems of low-income farmers and provides a basis for increased hope and confidence on the part of those millions of citizens of our country.

[Studies upon which legislation woud be based to carry out the above objectives had not been completed at the time this book went to press.—Ed.]

FEWER FARMERS—BIGGER SHARES [2]

United States farmers are within reach of a new and unexpected era of peacetime prosperity—with every prospect of an increase in individual farm incomes that will bring a rising standard of farm living regardless of Government price supports. . . .

A high and relatively level total of farm income is being divided up among fewer and fewer people living on farms. As a result, per capita farm income shows surprising strength, despite sharp drops in the prices of many farm products. . .

The real economic problem has always been the small, inefficient farmer—the man who has too little land to yield a good living, no matter how high prices might be. The real answer for him has always been a job in town. It's an answer

[2] From "Answer to the Farm Problem." *Business Week.* p23-4. April 2, 1955. Reprinted by permission.

to the "farm problem," too, because it leaves production for the market in the hands of his more efficient neighbors—and these more efficient farmers have usually been able to make a good living for themselves in all but the most severe depressions. . . .

Despite the subsidies . . . , the lure of jobs in town is always strong. In fact, it steadily outpulls the attractions of life on the farm—and . . . a sharp inroad is beginning to be made in the historic surplus of population on the farms. . . .

The 90 per cent support advocates . . . argue that farmers' income from the sale of products is sharply down and will drop still more under the Administration's flexible support plan. . . Farmers' net income from the sale of products dropped from $13.3 billion in 1953 to $12.0 billion in 1954. . . . [A further drop of over $1 billion in 1955 was reported by the Department of Agriculture.—Ed.]

But there is an offset to this argument, and the Administration is counting on it. Farmers' income from other sources besides the sale of products rose last year to $8.1 billion, a jump of $668 million.

The biggest part of this $8.1 billion comes from such sources as wages earned in off-farm jobs, dividends from stocks, and rents. Some of this does not go to actual farmers, of course; it includes people with substantial incomes from investments and salaries—and the incomes of many well-to-do businessmen who live on show places in the country. But it also includes a great many more people who work small farms and hold down modest jobs in town. . . .

The moral seems to be—to politicians as to businessmen—that the farm pocketbook is not geared so closely as it used to be to the price of such staples as hogs, poultry, and eggs.

The biggest single cause of the improved agricultural picture, in the opinion of key Administration officials, is the high level of business in general. You see one effect in the $8.1 billion that went to farmers last year from sources other than the sale of products.

You see another effect in the steady rise in consumption of meat, poultry, and dairy products. There has been a 12 per cent rise per capita in the use of livestock products since 1940—and the Administration wants to speed up this trend if possible.

But the major effect of booming business is the decline in farm population. When jobs are available, some farm people are always ready to sell out and move to town. For a time during the business downturn early last year, it looked as though the jobless would drift back in sufficient numbers to increase farm population. With the business rebound, the basic trend was resumed. Farm population dropped enough in 1954 to account for a rise in per capita farm income. . . .

The Administration . . . theory is that flexible supports will encourage farmers to make needed readjustments—such as going out of wheat and cotton and into more livestock production. Under flexible supports, the price support level on the stable field crops moves down, as surplus stocks increase.

At one time, it was hoped lower supports would result in less production. This hope has been given up.

But as a means of upgrading the United States diet, Administration thinkers believe flexible supports are here to stay.

A program to aid low-income farmers is expected to go to Congress this year. [See the preceding article, Secretary Benson's letter to the President.—Ed.]

Here's what Department of Agriculture officials have in mind: special credit programs and training for low-income farmers with the ability and ambition to get a real foothold in agriculture. Many will have to acquire larger farms than they now occupy. Other low-income farmers who would like to move to town would get help, too—perhaps through special job training courses.

The chief purpose, and the political selling point, will be relief of rural poverty. If the program takes hold, it will reduce the number of people now occupying about a million subsistence farms. Out of it will come more family-type commercial farms —and fewer farmers.

CAN THE FAMILY FARM BE SAVED? [3]

Will our farms of the future remain predominantly the family type—or are they going to follow the road that industry took many years ago toward large-scale, corporate operation?

You can't stir up much of a fuss when you ask people what the farm of the future *should be*. Politicians to a man, draw themselves up and heat the air with platitudes extolling the family farm as the backbone of America. Farm leaders firmly believe that agriculture must be kept in the hands of family operators—and are quick to remind you that their organizations give that aim the highest priority.

Even economists, who generally weigh values on the cold scales of efficiency, loosen up and express the hope that the powerful technical, social, and economic forces now changing the shape of agriculture at an increasing pace, won't divorce it from the traditional family-style. Some sociologists, however, raise the question as to whether it is the people, not the farm, in which we should be most interested. They suggest that as land becomes more scarce in relation to population, we may be forced in the national interest to move to different types of farming, whatever they may be.

We can take it for granted that this country *wants* to continue its unique family system of farming which up until the present has proved its ability to come through an astounding technical shake-up with its family colors still flying high.

Whether that desire will remain strong, nationally, while the farm population becomes a smaller and smaller part of our total United States people, is something that remains to be seen.

What we often overlook is the vital fact that the farm family did not accomplish its recent successful revolution strictly on its own resources, in a purely free-enterprise atmosphere. The family farm has had effective help from the rest of society, plenty of it, throughout United States history and has enjoyed

[3] From "The Family Farm Faces a Challenge," by John Bird, associate editor, *Country Gentleman. Country Gentleman.* 123:33+. November 1953. Reprinted by permission.

high favor in national policies. From early days, our national land policies encouraged settlement of our vast public domain in family units, not in the landlord-and-peasant estates that had been the rule in Europe.

The family farm had to have scientific research and education to become modern and to increase its efficiency—and you can't begin to measure the many ways in which it has been helped to adapt itself by the experiment stations, land-grant colleges, and the United States Department of Agriculture. All along the line the farmers' cooperatives and organizations have given the family-farm operator far greater bargaining power than he could hope to have as a lone individual in the markets and legislative halls. An important part of the picture, especially in recent decades, has been Government-sponsored farm credit systems especially designed to meet the needs of an expanding agriculture. The public stake in family-type agriculture has been recognized, too, in the various "action" farm programs which are supposed to provide the millions of independent farms with common means to adjust production to demand, to offset some of the income hazards farmers face, and to aid farmers in conserving soil and water resources.

How well the family farm maintains itself in the future— how successfully it goes through the major adjustments which seem to be ahead—depends to no small extent on the effectiveness of national farm policies and the programs and mechanisms the farmer uses.

There isn't any question that the public cost of most of these services has been a good bargain for the nation. Our family farming system has proved, in peace and war, in drought years and green years, that it can produce the abundance of food and fiber essential to our high standard of living. Never before has a country been blessed with such sustained plenty.

The last count of farms, the census of 1950, shows how strong the tide of change is running. We now have 5,382,000 farm units—or 1,066,000 less than thirty years ago. The largest farms have been growing the fastest, percentagewise. Since 1920, farms of 1000 acres or more have increased by 80 per cent. Farms of 500 acres and over have increased by 40 per cent.

Farms running 180 to 499 acres in size have remained about the same in numbers.

The big cut in farm numbers has come from consolidation of smaller units. Thirty years ago we had almost 3.5 million farms running from 10 to 99 acres; today we have 960,000 less, a loss of more than one in four. Where we had almost 1.5 million farms in the 100- to 179-acre class, we now have 187,000 fewer, a loss of about one in four. . . .

We've reached a point where fairly large farm operations —family-type or not—are the mainstay of our agriculture. . . . Class I farms—those producing $25,000 or more—average 2322 acres in size, and while they make up only 3.5 per cent of commercial farm numbers, they take up 24.5 per cent of the farm land and receive 26 per cent of total United States gross farm income. Class II farms—those with gross sales of $10,000 to $25,000—average 560 acres in size, number about 10 per cent of total commercial farms, take up 21 per cent of the farm-land, and produce 26 per cent of total gross farm income. . . .

The pattern of larger and larger farm enterprises holds plenty of problems for family-style operations. . . . Some farm leaders believe that the mushrooming needs of farmers for more capital, for more machines, more power and specialized managerial skills could prove to be the stumbling blocks for family operations. There have been few broad studies directly comparing large-scale farms with family-sized farms in efficiency, but much research does show that the larger, more specialized farm usually can produce at a lower cost per unit. . . .

However, the researchers don't give the large-scale farm all the advantages, by any means. One weak spot most of them see is the need of the large farm for hired labor. Nonfamily workers must be paid cash on the barrelhead. They work only a certain number of hours per day or week. They may not be available when most needed. All this means a loss in flexibility, in ability to make "spot" decisions which are such a factor in farming. Farm families can tighten their belts more easily when the going gets tough and cash is scarce, they can change plans quickly when need be, and the whole family—young and old—can work together when an emergency arises.

Overhead costs are another bugaboo of big farm operations. As one farmer-businessman told me, "When you get up toward ten hired men, you've got overhead problems. You add supervision costs. It keeps one man busy telling the others what to do. You get into expensive record-keeping. You find yourself tied down with an eight-hour day and a lot of standard rules—and agriculture doesn't always fit standard rules."

Because of these and other drawbacks, a number of economists believe that the law of diminishing returns sets in more quickly in agriculture than it does in industry, where materials and processes are more easily standardized. They believe that mere bigness loses its advantages in farming much farther down the scale than it does in manufacturing. They point out that the hazards of farming are great, and that the farm family can take losses "out of its hide," if necessary, which would wreck an industrial-type operation. A number of specialists who have studied the situation believe that, as a nation, we have much more to gain in agricultural stability and strength from consolidation of our too-small units into economic-size family farms than we can gain from an industrial-type farming system. They don't feel the farm situation is parallel with many lines of industry, where long ago efficiency demanded operations too large to be financed by the family, or too specialized and complex to be managed by an individual, bringing the age of the big corporations.

Just the same, if we want to make sure that our agriculture remains predominantly family-type, we must continue to make that goal a primary consideration in farm policies and programs. And many tried-and-true services and mechanisms used by agriculture need to be modernized or streamlined for future needs.

Some Extension Service officials, for example, . . . believe that as farms grow larger and more complex, the farmer needs training and technical assistance in developing complete, well-balanced management plans, each plan tailor-made for the individual farm. . . .

Others point out that rural youth training has become far more important than in the past, and needs new goals—not teaching young men and women how to become better farmers, but rather to give sound preparation to the majority of rural

youngsters who must seek their livelihood in business and industry. "There simply will be fewer places for them on farms,"
one official told me. "This country doesn't owe them or anybody else a living—but it does owe them equal opportunity."

The problem of larger capital requirements for those in
farming or who hope to become farmers is expected to become
more and more difficult. The farmer of a generation past, who
raised his own horsepower, horse feed, and used little commercial fertilizer, would be astonished and probably shocked at the
constant cash expense of farming today.

R. L. Farrington of the United States Department of Agricultural Credit Services, testifying before the House Committee
on Agriculture this year, brought out that the average investment
in a typical eastern Iowa farm went up from $39,420 in 1940,
to $90,703 in 1951. He cited a Minnesota study which showed
that between 1940 and 1949 the average capital required per
farm had doubled, cash farm operating expenses had multiplied
themselves five times. . . .

Farrington shelled it down to this: With the 1940 rate of
expenses, the average farmer could survive about nine years of
total loss of income before using up his entire capital—but at
the 1949 costs, it would take just four years to wipe him out.
Our national policies must recognize that a farm depression is a
far more deadly threat to the family farm than it was just a few
years ago. . . .

If our industrial economy continues to expand and opportunities are easy to find in the towns and cities, the trend toward
larger family farms—and some large-scale farms—will no doubt
continue full speed ahead. A depression could slow it down—
perhaps even bring a tide of jobless people seeking to ride
through a troubled time on the land. It depends, too, on whether
or not our national agricultural policies and programs keep the
family farm clearly in sight as a valued American institution to
be upheld, not just with kind words, but with modern scientific,
educational and economic facilities and services which will assist
the family farmer in holding his own in a fast-changing world.
The challenge boils down to this: How can the farm grow and
become more efficient, as it surely must, without losing its family
character?

VII. SUGGESTED PROGRAMS

EDITOR'S INTRODUCTION

The final section of this book is devoted to programs suggested by economic research groups. Each is more or less a one-package prescription for treating all of agriculture's ills. The diagnoses and proposed remedies reflect the diverse viewpoints of these groups, but all have the same objective: a stable and vigorous agricultural economy.

In the first of these extracts, the Farm Foundation turns "the searchlight on farm policy." A committee composed wholly of agricultural economists examines the successes and mistakes of the past to chart a course for the future.

The Research and Policy Committee of the Committee for Economic Development addresses itself to what it regards as three fundamental weaknesses: overproduction, instability of farm income, and inadequacy of resources for many farm families. The members of this study group represent business, finance, and industry.

The Conference on Economic Progress offers a blueprint for "economic justice for farmers," "abundance" for all Americans, and "enough food" for the free world. The group preparing this report included leaders of farm organizations, labor union officials, former New Deal economists and a sprinkling of business executives.

Finally, the National Planning Association lists and describes policies that it believes deserve to be tested in pilot projects. This statement was drawn up by the Association's board of directors and members of its Business, Labor and International Committees.

THE LESSONS OF THE PAST [1]

We believe that twelve conclusions are clearly indicated by the record [of farm-support programs since 1929].

(1) A public policy of economic "equality for agriculture" as compared with other parts of the economy commends itself to American thinking—off the farm as well as on. Furthermore, there is widespread agreement that in the early twenties agriculture was disadvantaged to a degree that some kind of public action was warranted and, indeed, in the general interest. Similar circumstances arose during the thirties and may again in the future. The basic issue in this area relates, therefore, not so much to the question of desirable objectives, but to the question of what constitutes equality for agriculture and how best to achieve it. . . .

(2) The term "parity" and the arithmetic formulas in which it has been computed do not well express this goal of equality for agriculture. The ratio of prices received by the farmer for his commodities and prices paid by him for farm and home supplies during the five-year period 1909-1914 bears no clear or significant relationship to the economist's idea of equilibrium returns to labor, management, and capital in various farm and nonfarm uses. . . .

Even if these prices were in an economically desirable relationship in this five-year period before World War I, the use of the same formula four decades later would not promote a satisfactory functioning of the economy unless conditions of technology, market demand, and other economic factors had remained unchanged, or unless changes had affected all the prices and qualities in substantially the same way. This is clearly not true in a dynamic society such as ours. . . .

If the programs move closer to parity of real income as between farmers and nonfarmers, this would mean progress in the direction implied by the concept of parity. However, if the effort to equalize incomes of the two groups takes the form of continuous cash supplements or subsidies rather than returns from

[1] From "Turning the Searchlight on Farm Policy," pamphlet. Conference Committee, The Farm Foundation. 600 South Michigan Avenue. Chicago 5. 1952. p32-52. Reprinted by permission.

the market, this means that resources, especially labor resources, are being used in agriculture when they could be used more profitably in other lines. . . .

(3) The record shows that the real objective of farm policies and farm programs has been higher prices or higher incomes as such. It has not been the achievement of any carefully measured equality which, if attained, would be stable because economically sound. . . .

High farm prices have been confused with agricultural prosperity. A rigid price structure has been confused with stability of the economy. It would be more true to say that striving for high price supports has resulted in misuse of the "parity" label than to say that the parity idea itself has been responsible for pressure to get high prices.

(4) The quest for prices maintained above the trend of market values leads to undue reliance on organizational power and political pressures. This tends to lessen the farmers' drive toward economically desirable adjustments of their industry (or component parts of it) to the other parts of our economy. It may even weaken the motive to make maximum improvement in operating efficiency. . . .

(5) If farm prices are supported at a higher level than that which the market would establish, control of production or/and marketing or use, will have to be instituted in the effort to keep prices up to this artificial level. Those controls often rely on voluntary enforcement at the start but move inevitably toward compulsory controls and substantial restriction of the farmer's freedom of choice. . . .

(6) Production controls are ineffective if applied to a limited range of products and therefore tend to spread. If farmers are restricted in acreage of specified crops, they select their best acres, apply more fertilizer, and give better care to the crops so that outputs prove to be less than proportionately reduced. Idle acres are put into nonrestricted crops. The administrative or legislative authority is prone to meet this situation by extending the list of controlled commodities. . . . The control machinery becomes more complicated, costs to the Federal Treasury greatly increase.

(7) The storage program turns into a device for supporting prices above their free market level even in times of full employment and abundant purchasing power. The history of the stabilization corporations under the Farm Board and of storage operations under the Agricultural Adjustment Act and subsequent legislation shows that it is very easy to withdraw commodities from the market as a means of raising prices but difficult or impossible to liquidate these stocks in accordance with any economically sound plan of "orderly marketing" or production adjustment. Sale of government stocks will take place only in periods of extraordinary demand, particularly wartime. Extensive storage in peacetime thus is costly and contributes to generally inflationary movements. It is impossible to achieve a useful or even a defensible storage program by using "parity" as the criterion for withdrawing stocks from the market. . . .

(8) Continuous price support at high levels does not safeguard against the swings of the business cycle. Booms lead to depressions, and a general business depression is the most serious economic threat the farmer has to face, since it undermines both consumer and industrial demand for his product. . . .

Since agriculture must continuously adjust to changing situations, a program that is rigid and mechanistic does not stabilize but rather has the opposite effect. Use of the parity formula may produce practically the same dollar and cents price per unit in years of big crops as in years of small crops. From the farm income standpoint, this is definitely unstabilizing and, moreover, tends to impede the adjustments needed to correct over- and under-production. Furthermore, it creates situations in which large accumulations, or oversupplies of given farm products may bring on eventually a disastrous break in the agricultural price structure as a whole. . . .

(9) Farm policy should be an integral part of the general stabilization efforts of business and of Government. Dealing with agriculture in a vacuum, disregarding what is happening in other parts of the economy and the impact of farm programs on nonfarm business, will not bring stable prosperity to farmers. . . .

Farmers must face the consequences to the country which follow heavy financial drafts on the Treasury in support of farm programs. They must be concerned about monetary policies and the proper exercise of credit management, both farm and non-farm, as a means of checking inflationary tendencies and preserving the solvency and stability of their own enterprises and also of the commercial and financial agencies with which they deal. They must, in the broadest sense, face the problems of debt management and taxation (including a willingness to bear an equitable share of the burden) since the health of the economy as a whole is essential to farm prosperity.

(10) Farm policy should consider international as well as national issues and objectives. If prices are maintained above the free market level, the result will be to attract products from other countries. This gives rise to pressure for curbs on imports in order to maintain these prices and to keep other countries from sharing in them. Such efforts to maintain arbitrarily high prices lead toward economic nationalism. Sale for export is made more difficult. Export subsidies may be resorted to and these may lead to retaliation from abroad. Therefore, high price supports are inconsistent with our national aim of promoting international cooperation.

(11) A number of policies other than price support make important contributions toward the built-in stability of agriculture and to the farmer's ability to prosper through his own efforts. . . .

The improvement of rural credit institutions since 1916 is a good illustration. When a farmer holds his productive plant subject to a three-year real estate mortgage or perhaps even a one-year chattel mortgage, a relatively short period of unfavorable yields or depressed markets can cripple his business. With ample credit now available under long-term amortized mortgages, the commercial farmer is in a better position to operate on the law of averages and, with reasonably good management, can weather the ordinary short-term business risk. . . .

(12) The fact that farming is still a small-scale and high risk industry must be taken into account in future policy making. . . . Technology has given the farmer somewhat greater control over physical and biological processes, and the advance of

farm management has brought better business administration. During recent years of farm prosperity, there has been great reduction in farm debt and substantial accumulation of financial reserves. On the other hand, the switch from draft animals to gasoline and electric power, increasing reliance on purchased fertilizers and insecticides, the rise in taxes and in the price of hired farm labor have given the farmer a high break-even point and made him financially more vulnerable. . . . The industry has a unique need for governmental protection against the dangers of general depression. . . .

To shape farm policy constructively to the future needs of the country, we need to study carefully where present trends are pointing rather than merely projecting the patterns of past thinking. . . .

In marked contrast to the weak economic position and the depressed conditions out of which our present farm legislation emerged, it appears that the outlook for American agriculture during the next five or ten years, and probably longer, is basically strong. . . .

The circumstances which led to the agricultural depression of the twenties and thirties included . . . widespread and profound changes in the conditions of agricultural demand and supply. . . .

One effect of World War I was that Great Britain and several continental countries that had formerly furnished important consumer and industrial markets for American supplies of food, fiber and tobacco seek a greater degree of self-sufficiency or "Imperial preference" in their sources of these products. By raising protective tariff rates, our Congress made it still more difficult for other countries to export their industrial products to us and thus pay for agricultural imports. . . .

Between World War I and World War II, the farmer had also to contend with certain adverse demand factors in his domestic market. There was a short but sharp business recession in 1920-1921 and severe industrial depression following the crash of 1929. These seriously impaired the ability of our city populations to buy agricultural products. The situation was further complicated by the substitution of synthetic products of nonfarm origin for leather, textile fibers, and other products which were important items in our farm market. While some enthusiasts looked to industrial chemistry to furnish important new markets for farm products, results in this direction were relatively minor.

. . . [Another] factor undermining the demand for agricultural products came in part from the farm itself. This was the rapid switch from horses and mules to gasoline- and electricity-driven equipment. This change reduced the number of horses and mules on farms from 26.7 million in 1918 to 14.4 million in 1940. This sharply curtailed horse-raising as a farm enterprise and released some 60 million acres of land from production of feeds for draft animals to other productive uses. At the same time, the total power resources added to agriculture were enormous. Moreover the power-driven equipment added greatly to the efficiency of production and to the abilty of farmers to overcome adverse weather conditions. Thus this factor operated not merely to reduce demands for farmers' output but also to increase its supply.

. . . There were other factors tending to enlarge the supply of farm products on a market already weak. Notable was the expansionary effect of broader adoption of improved farming techniques. . . .

While it is certain that progress both in equipment and farming methods will continue, the revolutionary impact of cheap and flexible farm power has been quite fully assimilated within the structure of our agricultural-industrial relations. Some of the other factors which hit agriculture simultaneously with mechanization seem to have spent their greatest force or actually to have been reversed.

This is notably true as to the upward trend of population growth which appears to be much broader than a mere war phenomenon or a merely American manifestation. If a high level of employment at good wages is maintained, the recent tendency to early and fruitful marriages will probably be continued. Paralleling the upward trend of population is a significant tendency toward mobilizing the resources of the free world to aid the recovery of those who bore the brunt of World War II and of reviving and accelerating the progress of underdeveloped nations within the circle of the free world. . . .

The industrial growth of the United States, plus the export demands of two world wars, has resulted in considerable attrition of various resources of which we originally had an abundant home supply. This makes it necessary to enlarge our imports of many raw materials, and this in turn gives foreign exporters a purchasing power which will, both directly and indirectly, sustain a substantial market for American farm products.

Reinforcing this tendency toward economic expansion, there is a world-wide movement toward positive programs to safeguard national economies and the world economy against tragic and unnecessary depressions which have been experienced in the past. . . . [Such] policies are being undertaken in other countries, and attempts are being made to link these efforts with a view of promoting stability internationally. . . .

An inflationary boom is a discernible prospect in the economic world in which the agricultural industry must function within the next decade or so. Both logic and history indicate that a runaway boom invites disastrous recession. Hence an adequate and permanent national farm policy should be designed to keep agriculture from aggravating inflation and to permit it to exercise the anti-inflationary influence of efficient competition. . . .

Over a large part of the country, the farm has ceased to be a self-sufficient unit. The living of its members has become more completely dependent on cash income from the market, and the farmer has also to meet larger seasonal and even week-by-week demands for cash operating expense, such as gasoline, oil, commercial feeds, pedigreed or hybrid seed, and fertilizer. The disastrous consequences of a sharp fall in market prices tend to hit farmers more promptly and severely than under the more primitive and self-sufficing types of agriculture.

On the other hand, as has also been pointed out, the credit facilities—both long-term and short-term—which assist the farmer in meeting and riding through periods of strain have been greatly improved. An important contributing factor in the depressions of the early twenties and thirties was a weak banking structure. . . . We now have also the Federal Deposit Insurance Corporation with its strong reserves.

Furthermore, there has been an unprecedented accumulation of liquid assets by many farmers during more than a decade of prosperous years. Farmers today are more adequately insured, have larger bank accounts, and hold more Government bonds and private securities than ever in the past. Hence, Government maintenance of prices at high levels or subsidizing the farmer for losses which grow out of average risks inherent in the industry is not demanded of a sound national farm policy.

Finally, the increase in supplementary sources of income to farm families may be expected to continue in the future. In many parts of the country, the families that live on small, low-producing farms are less dependent on the farm alone for their living than was true a couple of decades ago. The tendency for many industries to decentralize into smaller communities, the growth of a variety of service industries associated with modern mechanization, and the opportunity for seasonal employment on near-by commercial farms provide increasing opportunities for farm families on small or low-producing farms to supplement their farm incomes. Ignoring these supplementary sources of income when presenting statistics of "average" farm income has frequently created the impression that the farm problem is more serious or different in character from what it actually is. To the extent that industrialization of rural areas and the trend toward more nonfarm sources of income continues, there will be less need for remedial income programs directed at this group of "farm people."

THREE FUNDAMENTAL PROBLEMS [2]

Behind the complexity and diversity of American agriculture, and the painful symptoms of maladjustment which currently afflict it, the Committee [for Economic Development] believes there are three fundamental problems.

[2] From "Economic Policy for American Agriculture," pamphlet. Research and Policy Committee, Committee for Economic Development. 444 Madison Avenue. New York 22. p33-5. January 1956. Reprinted by permission.

(1) There is too much production of some farm products. Wheat is the most troublesome. In response to the needs of World War II and the postwar relief period, output increased by almost 50 per cent. While output has been curtailed in recent years, it is still in excess of normal peacetime requirements, and further reduction therefore is necessary. There is also a surplus of cotton large enough to require a major reduction of output. Corn and the other feed grains are produced in excess of current needs, but the problem here appears easier to solve; while production should be curtailed moderately for a time, growing demand for livestock products will probably close the gap between unrestricted production and consumption within a few years.

(2) Farmers' incomes are highly unstable. Sometimes incomes are unstable because of variations in yields due to natural causes such as the weather and disease. Sometimes fluctuations occur because of variations in demand. These fluctuations are larger than necessary to stimulate appropriate adjustments and they cause serious hardship to farm families.

(3) Many full-time farm families have too few resources to permit a satisfactory income. This problem chiefly concerns about one million farmers, mostly in the South.

Despite the urgency of these problems, many farmers are in a sound economic position. In particular, the operators of many commercial family farms have incomes roughly comparable to those of nonfarm people, though they have not gained as much in recent years. More than half of farm products as measured by their market value have no price supports at all. Land prices are back to their peak levels of 1952, and the farmers' debt situation is generally sound.

The economic good health of large sections of agriculture is due in great measure to the high general level of activity in the United States during the past fifteen years, and to the steady decline in the farm population during that period. Over the past five years about one million persons a year have been leaving agriculture, the workers in this group finding other occupations. This trend must be continued if we are to solve the underlying problems, because farmers increase productivity more rapidly than consumption of food is increased.

The basic defects of high price supports as a solution to agriculture's troubles have been revealed by experience. High supports encourage excess production, which leads to acreage allotments and marketing quotas. But farmers eventually succeed in increasing output even on the smaller number of acres allotted them, and surpluses become unmanageable. In addition, it is doubtful whether high price supports actually increase net income per farm family over a period of years. It is clear that they do not contribute much to relieve the problem of the low-income farmers, since these farmers produce little for market.

A return to a free market for agricultural products is proposed by some. The Committee believes free markets generally are the most efficient method of keeping production and use geared together, but experience has shown that farmers suffer unduly from the wide price swings which are characteristic of free markets for agricultural products. Devices to check sharp and temporary price declines should be sought.

Solutions to the basic problems of agriculture should follow these lines:

To determine key matters of policy as far removed as possible from political pressures, an Agricultural Stabilization Board should be set up, with the Secretary of Agriculture as its chairman.

To deal with the problem of surpluses, . . . [the Committee] believes it is necessary to reduce the amount of resources, especially manpower, now devoted to production of some crops, and that the community as a whole should help farmers bear the cost of this adjustment. A land retirement program is recommended which will allow some land now in wheat to revert to grazing. It may also be necessary to withold from cultivation some land now used for cotton and the production of feed crops. At the same time the support prices of wheat, cotton and the feed grains should be gradually reduced to the level at which production and demand are in balance and some of the surpluses now on hand can be moved into consumption. During this period, it would be desirable to retain acreage allotments and market quotas. The goal at the end of the adjustment period, which would last perhaps five years, is to make it possible for farmers to earn satisfactory incomes without depending on Government purchases or production controls.

Greater income stability can be achieved in part through a storage system operated in such a way as to iron out fluctuations in net returns to farmers due to variations in yields. When fluctuations are due to temporary declines in consumption, two courses are possible. The government may support prices and withhold some stocks from immediate consumption. Or prices may be allowed to seek their own level and government payments made to farmers to supplement their incomes. Payments would be based on the difference between the prevailing market price and what the price would normally be in a period of high employment and normal yield. More important than the choice of the method to be used in moderating fluctuations is the level at which prices or incomes will be supported. The goal should be to prevent wide or sustained departure from the long-run free market level. Support levels could be determined either by formulae included in the basic legislation, or by the proposed nonpartisan Agricultural Stabilization Board.

The problems of low-income farmers may be alleviated by stimulating trends already in existence. The movement of people out of farming in the South, where the low-income farmers are largely concentrated, has been more rapid than in the rest of agriculture. This movement should be encouraged by increasing the amount of information available about jobs in urban areas. The possibilities of offering financial aid to families who want to move and of encouraging industrialization in rural areas should also be explored. Farmers who remain in the low-income areas should be assisted in obtaining larger farms; for this, special credit arrangements and training in new methods will be required in many cases.

There is no quick and easy way out of our present farm difficulties. But the direction in which we must proceed is clear. The consumer who is interested in efficient production of food and fibers, the taxpayer who has to pay the cost of losses due to high price support policies, the farmer who wants to earn a higher and more stable income, will all benefit from solutions of agriculture's problems on a basis consistent with the fullest development of a free enterprise economy under which all elements contribute to the most efficient use of human and material resources. There is a national responsibility to help agriculture reach such solutions.

FIVE DEFICIENCIES IN POLICIES [3]

The main deficiencies in current farm policies and programs are: First, expansion of consumption at home and abroad, as a constructive approach, has been inadequately dealt with; second, attempts to adjust production have been piecemeal and inconsistent and have generated larger maladjustments and "surpluses"; third, the treatment of farm income has put this vital element last instead of first, dealt with it unsympathetically, and accelerated the downward trend; fourth, the problem of poverty, so highly concentrated in farm areas, has been virtually overlooked; and fifth, no systematic efforts are being made to facilitate on favorable terms the inevitable exodus from agriculture, which may reach about 2 million people within the next five years. These . . . related elements of farm policies and programs need to be drastically revised.

The Government should develop immediate and long-range 1956-1960 estimates for domestic consumption and export of farm products. The ultimate purpose of production is to serve consumers. Without appropriate levels of domestic and export consumption as a guide, farm production "adjustments" are now being made in the dark. . . .

Full consumption of farm products depends upon a full economy. Even now, despite high prosperity, there are substantial soft spots. And with our productive potential advancing so rapidly, expanded or new measures are needed to keep consumption in line with productive ability. . . .

Special measures should be adopted to enlarge consumption by low-income families.

[3] From "Full Prosperity for Agriculture." Conference on Economic Progress. 1001 Connecticut Avenue. Washington 6, D.C. November 1955. p92-104. Reprinted by permission.

This includes consideration of various subsidy proposals, which now have important sponsorship in the Congress, to distribute food to needy consumers on relief or receiving very low incomes, and expansion of the school lunch program. Programs of this type should in 1960 add almost a billion dollars to the annual level of consumer food expenditures, but the immediate need is much larger, with more "surpluses" and more low-income families than there should be in 1960. Since the consumer subsidies for these purposes would be largely to pay the Government for "surplus" stock, the net cost to the Government would be much less than the size of the subsidies.

Export consumption should be lifted sharply and immediately by measures to enlarge trade and by some expansion of United States financial assistance.

There should be long-range United States participation in the Reciprocal Trade Agreements program, accompanied by further lowering of tariff barriers in return for trade concessions abroad. We should simplify customs procedure, and join the Organization for Trade Cooperation. Careful consideration should be given to the proposal by a bipartisan group of more than twenty United States senators to establish an International Food and Raw Materials Reserve. The United States should also facilitate a larger flow of private capital into foreign development fields by lowering the tax rate on foreign investments and by permitting the deferment of the tax until the income earned in other countries is actually brought back to this country. These measures should accomplish, through regular commercial channels, somewhat more than three quarters of the total desired level of farm product exports in 1960. . . .

With consumption goals as a guide, the Government should develop immediate and long-range 1956-1960 coordinated estimates for desirable adjustments in farm production, and encouragement of actual adjustments should he harmonized rather than made piecemeal. . . .

The current "surpluses" should be separated from the general problem of farm production adjustment. These "surpluses" should be worked down to the level of adequate food and fiber reserves . . . special consumer programs for low-income groups, undertaken immediately in larger magnitudes than will be needed at 1960 income levels in an expanded economy. The "surpluses" should also be worked down by vigorous disposal programs overseas to needy consumers in underdeveloped areas. . . . Simultaneously, the current and future size and composition of farm production should be adjusted as closely as feasible to sustainable consumer markets in a full employment environment plus a sustainable level of exports. . . .

The soil conservation program should be strengthened, along with programs for flood control and forestry. Payments should be made to farmers to improve and conserve acreage withdrawn from cultivation, which may total about 8.5 million acres by 1960. But unless these payments are of a size geared to appropriate goals for farm income, any such program would compound the defects of current programs, which use both acreage restrictions and lower price supports to force farm income downward, and also drive farmers into unrestrained production along undesirable lines. To maintain sufficient food and fiber reserves requires adequate storage of nonperishables. . . . Production . . . should be high enough to guard against miscalculation, natural calamity, and even the possibility of international conflict. . . .

All farm production policies should be closely geared to farm income policies.

Farmers suffering from economic injustice or poverty cost the nation far more than farm "surpluses." If we seek the best farm production adjustments consistent with sound farm income adjustments, we shall do far better in all respects than if we try to make farm production adjustments with disregard for the impact upon the lives and livelihoods of farmers. . . .

As a guide to all farm policies, the Government should establish immediate and long-range 1956-1960 goals for the expansion of farm income, designed ultimately to lift it toward parity with the incomes of the nonfarm population. . . . Whatever method is used, the objectives should be in terms of farm income—not just price.

The traditional methods of protecting farm income need improvement, with use of both price supports and income payments. . . .

To lift total farm income derived from farming in 1956 to a fair minimum target of about $2 billion above 1954, and to at least $3 billion above the severely depressed mid-1955 annual rate, price supports would be required on most major commodities at a level averaging about 90 per cent of parity as traditionally measured, accompanied by adjustments in production plus programs to expand domestic consumption and exports in a full employment environment.

This would meet the emergency problem in 1956, and allow time to shift toward an improved long-range approach, designed to lift total farm income derived from farming to about $22.5 billion by 1960, or about 70 per cent above the mid-1955 level of about $13.2 billion. Even then, the per capita income of the farm population, including income derived from nonfarm sources, would still be only about two thirds of nonfarm per capita income in 1960 in a full economy.

This longer-range approach should continue to benefit by the tested device of price supports, especially in the case of storable commodities, but should seek to go all the way toward the establishment of a modern and realistic base period than the years 1910-14. In addition, this longer-range approach should make substantial use of income payments. The objective for each of the various farm commodities should always be set in terms of income, whether price supports by Government loans and purchases, or income payments, or in some instances a workable combination of these two methods, are used to achieve the income objective. Income payments, where used, would pay the difference between the market price per unit sold and the return to the farmer consistent with the income objective. . . .

The Government's immediate and long-range 1956-1960 objectives for expanding farm income should contain specific targets and programs for the reduction of farm poverty, and for strengthening the family-type farm. . . .

Farm price supports and income payments should help to narrow the gap between poverty and high incomes in agriculture, and to strengthen the family-type farm.

In 1953, 1.9 per cent of the farmers received 25 per cent of the income benefits derived from price supports; 9 per cent of the farmers got half of these benefits; and 91 per cent got the other half. This served further to distort the distribution of farm income. To reverse this trend, after the objectives for farm income for any commodity have been set, the assistance to help achieve these objectives might be so scaled as to point most of the benefits to those who need them most. This would give higher priority to the liquidation of farm poverty and the strengthening of the family-type farm, rather than to the further enlargement of high incomes or large farms. . . .

The family-type farm should be further strengthened by improved credit facilities, and by encouragement of farm cooperatives.

The Farm Credit Administration should be enabled to provide more abundant credit on improved terms to the family farm. Further to improve the productivity of these farms, the program of the Rural Electrification Administration should also be enlarged. To enable more submarginal farmers to become family-type farmers, the rehabilitation and tenant purchase loan program of the Farmers Home Administration should be augmented. Consideration should also be given to such proposals as those embodied in the Marketing Facilities Improvement Bill.

In 1952, 10,000 farm purchasing and marketing cooperatives, with about 7 million farmer members, were doing an annual business of about $9 billion. Nearly one quarter of all farm products move through cooperative channels at some stage, and the percentage is considerably higher for some commodities, such as dairy products. . . . The equity of farmers in cooperatives rose from less than $1 billion in 1940 to $3 billion by the end of 1954. Pending restrictive tax legislation on their operations should not be enacted. The Farmer Cooperative Service of the United States Department of Agriculture should be expanded and encouraged to disseminate information about cooperatives to the general public. The Farm Credit Administration, through its Bank for Cooperatives, should be granted wider discretion in making loans to cooperatives, particularly in the difficult stage of initial organization. The cooperative machinery could also be used more effectively, with proper encouragement, to establish yardsticks for lower-cost electric power, to provide medical services, to finance farm housing, and for consumer credit unions. . . .

Between now and 1960, about 750,000 farm family workers and hired farm workers, comprising about 2 million people when their families are included, need to shift from full-time or part-time farm work to full-time employment outside of agriculture. . . . The proper way to make this adjustment in resource use is not to force more and more of the farm population downward to lower levels of income, but rather to provide opportunity for most of those who are already at these low levels to move into useful and rewarding work outside of agriculture. . . .

Outlays toward the well-being of agriculture have never been maintained at anywhere near a parity ratio with public outlays to protect and advance the fair interests of other segments of the economy. Moreover, the lifting of farm income would not be a net cost to our economy; it would represent a gain in real output, in levels of consumption for the whole population, in standards of living, and above all in the extension of justice to the farm population. . . .

The total outlays by the Federal Government for agriculture and for an adequate level of food consumption would not average more than in the neighborhood of 4 to 5 per cent of the total Federal Budget, not high when measured against the need. The proposed outlays in the form of United States financial assistance to other countries, in order to help meet pressing food needs, would be in an annual amount tapering off to about $2 billion by 1960, but somewhat higher in the intervening years. About half of this would be loans, so that the grant figure would be only about two thirds as high as the grant figure in 1954. While this program would benefit American farmers, just as American military aid to other countries benefits American manufacturers, its real purpose is to support a sound international economic policy. Consequently, by no means all of this cost should be classified as cost of the farm program. It should be noted, however, that annual outlays for this purpose, only about $500 million higher in 1960 than in 1954 even including repayable loans, in an economy with an annual output about $130 billion higher at full employment, would be a very modest and sustainable contribution toward the common purposes of the free world.

WHAT POLICIES MERIT A TRIAL? [4]

In the general debate about current farm problems, we should remember that there is now and has been for a number of years wide agreement in this nation on the basic elements of farm policy. Most people now agree that we must conserve our soil and water resources, do something to reduce price instability in agriculture, maintain adequate national reserves of food and fiber, and keep farm income at a level comparable with the income of the rest of the economy. The debate now is largely in terms of how fast, how much, what level, what method. . . .

What kinds of farm policies have general acceptance? What possible developments in these policies should be tried out on a pilot scale? . . .

Maintain farming as a sound national industry. Measured against the demand now in sight, we have and will continue to have excess capacity in agriculture in the short run—excess acres, excess labor and even excess farmers, and also such things as excess machinery and fertilizer. During the immediate period when the squeeze of rising costs and falling prices may be most severe, it is important that our national farm policy take a long view with the basic objective of maintaining a healthy and sound agriculture. Farm income, therefore, must be maintained at a level of parity to nonfarm incomes. The areas of disagreement concern levels, methods of supports, and particularly products to be covered.

[4] From "A New Look at Farm Policy," a statement by the Agriculture Committee on National Policy, National Planning Association. 1601 New Hampshire Avenue. Washington 9, D.C. January 1956. p9-40. Reprinted by permission.

Conserve and use wisely our soil and water resources. . . .
Effective programs aimed at genuine conservation reduce production temporarily, but tend to increase production in the long
run. For the next few years, emphasis should be placed on those
conservation practices that truly conserve and yet do not result
in immediate increase in output. Higher priority in use of public
funds should be placed on such practices as returning marginal
crop land to permanent vegetation, shifting from row crops to
grasses, reducing livestock on some depleted western ranges,
zoning and rearrangement of cropping patterns.

Much lower priority should be placed on reclaiming or
bringing new lands into irrigation. Projects should be dropped
entirely in areas where constructing irrigation facilities will cost
taxpayers generally more than the value of the added land.

Keep farm prices realistic. Farm prices are a means and not
an end in themselves. There is a tendency in recent years to
overemphasize what can be accomplished by changing price
support levels. . . . Only in a few cases are present price support
levels seriously out of line with reality. In some instances, price
supports at too high levels have accentuated the tendency for
production to outrun markets, but the fundamental causes for
this constantly expanding farm output lies outside the framework
of farm prices.

Reduce price instability. The price uncertainties of agriculture
are lessened by steady employment and heavy payrolls in industry, hence the farm need for a healthy total economy is great.
Apparently the economy outside agriculture can get along for a
short time even if farmers are in trouble. However, it is in the
long-run interest of labor, business, and consumer for the agricultural economy to be sound and prosperous so that needed food
and fiber can be produced efficiently and so that farm people can
earn enough to purchase their share of the output of our rapidly
expanding industrial economy. . . .

We must continue to test measures that will reduce this price
instabilty in agriculture, while retaining the national benefit of
stable and liberal farm production. We have provided some
price stability in major crops through commodity loans. Live-

stock producers who also face problems of price instability are assisted only indirectly by supports on feed grains.

Nevertheless, we need to experiment with supports at moderate levels for livestock products begininning with one product— milk, for instance. . . . Such supports should be backed by production payments [i.e., direct payments to the farmer when the market price is lower than the support price], not by purchase and storage.

Maintain national reserves. The nation has always lived on scant margins and has hoped that we might get a lucky break on the weather. World War II provided a good example of inadequate reserves. Although these reserves looked big at the time, they let us slide through only because we happened to be blessed with good crop years. . . .

Without a firm, long-term program we swing between two extreme positions. When food and fibers are critical and vital to the national interest, for example during war or widespread drought, we deplore the lack of reserve stocks and initiate programs to build them up. But when the reserves in the granary build up, we are alarmed at the cost of storage and rotation of stocks. . . .

Certainly a program for holding strategic reserves of food and fibers should not be used as a price support measure. On the other hand, policy on reserve stocks should be firm, stable, and widely understood. Such stocks must be insulated from the market. . . .

Increase domestic consumption. . . . One of the keys to the long-run solution of the basic problem in agriculture—the tendency for production to outrun markets—is the increased domestic consumption of animal products. There are two reasons for this. First, an increase in consumption of animal products would improve general nutrition and it would meet consumers' wants. Second, it would help reduce surplus production because an acre of wheat or cotton or corn shifted to forage crops and finally marketed as animal products slows down production substantially. . . .

Following are four examples of programs for increasing domestic food consumption which should be developed as soon as possible.

(a) Domestic food allotment (food stamp plan). This kind of approach has strong support. We had limited experience with a similar program during the 1930's. We need to put such a program into operation immediately on a pilot basis in selected areas or cities. The cost would not be great, and it would provide answers as to the feasibility of a larger scale program.

Food stamps would be issued to low income people. Included in this group should be those now on relief, those on Federal and state old-age assistance, and perhaps persons now receiving unemployment compensation. Priority should be given to areas or cities where unemployment is a problem. . . .

Food would be distributed through regular channels. At the present time, stamps should be used only for foods in surplus and especially for animal products.

(b) Production payments. At present, dairy products are supported by purchase and storage at 75 per cent of parity. This involves complicated handling and storage charges, followed by resale at low prices or by handouts. An opportunity is offered here to try out production payments as a substitute for purchase and storage. Under production payments, the market would set the price and the Government would make up to the farmer the difference between the market and the support price. Such an experiment with dairy products would throw light on the two methods of support and would indicate which would be more desirable in case support of other livestock products seemed to be desirable in the future.

(c) Milk products. The use of production payments . . . would be a substitute for the present purchase and storage methods. But milk products also require a fundamental change in the long-standing method of pricing which overvalues milk fat compared with nonfat milk solids. . . .

One method of accomplishing this shift might be to provide income payments to dairy producers on butterfat for a period of, say nine years. During the first three years, payments could be based on 75 per cent of the current price, the second three years 50 per cent, the third three years 25 per cent and after that no payment. . . .

(d) School lunch program. This program now reaches only about 30 per cent of our children. . . . Vigorous steps should be taken to increase participation for at least 75 per cent of the children. . . . .

Maintain and increase foreign demand. . . . Vigorous efforts should be made to sell our farm products in the world markets through normal channels. As an elementary first step, necessary revision should be made in trade practice regulations so as to insure high quality in American products being traded.

Food and fiber reserves are not only important as a safeguard against possible war; they are a tool to prevent war. Such products as wheat and dry nonfat solids can and should be distributed outside normal trade channels in troubled areas around the world. These surpluses may be sold for foreign currencies, or in some cases donated, to meet human needs and to promote economic development abroad. Such programs must support our over-all foreign policy and avoid simply dumping American food abroad. . . .

Shift production. The most urgent adjustment involves wheat, of which we now have a two-year supply. Under the allotment and marketing quota program, a substantial reduction already has been made in wheat acreage. The acreage harvested in 1954 was 12 million less than the 1943-52 average. The 1955 wheat quotas called for another 7-million-acre cut. In fact, the 55-million-acre planting for 1955 was 20 million less than the average acreage planted in the postwar years. Even with this reduction in wheat acreage, further downward adjustment will be necessary if wheat surpluses continue to build up. . . .

Additional acres taken out of wheat should be planted to soil-holding crops. More cotton acres need to be shifted to grass. Eventually, some of these soil-holding grasses and legumes could be utilized for livestock products.

As a means of holding livestock expansion in check, some shifts from feed grains to forage production should also be encouraged. Increased acreage of soil-holding crops would both reduce soil losses and keep the supply of livestock feed from being as burdensome.

Following are three examples of new approaches that should be tested out on a pilot basis as aids in reducing production of surplus crops. These programs would not require large budgets. Only a very small portion of funds now allotted for price supports would be ample.

(a) Soil bank (conservation reserve). . . . We must develop means to store our excess capacity in the soil and have it there for future need rather than to produce crops that we do not need at home and cannot sell abroad.

(b) Land retirement. In some high-risk areas, such as the Dust Bowl section, wheat is about the only cash crop worth while to the operator. It doesn't make sense to suggest that he shift to some other crop. The Department of Agriculture should try out pilot programs for leasing or purchasing some of this marginal wheat land and retiring it from production for some years but with eventual use as pasture for cattle in mind. . . . The payments to the operator under the lease should cover costs of establishing cover to prevent soil blowing. Such leased acreages could be returned to production before the expiration of the lease in case of national emergency.

(c) Grass seed. The relatively large investment in seed, in addition to lime and fertilizer, needed to establish stands of legumes and grasses slows down the shift from wheat, cotton, and corn to soil-holding crops. Last spring it cost approximately $6 for seed to sow one acre of grass and legume forage. The Department of Agriculture should provide for additional research in seed production. Price supports should be provided for grass and legume seeds in years of excess production. Since large and more stable supplies of such seeds are essential for a general shift to soil-holding and forage crops, it may be necessary to provide direct payments to seed growers for expanded production.

It should be noted that successful programs for shifting acres to soil-holding crops will probably increase livestock production before many years. Taken alone, this merely shifts the burden of the surplus problem to the back of the livestock producer. Such shift production policy makes sense only if the nation maintains a full-employment economy and, in addition, supports vigorously a corollary policy for increasing domestic consumption.

Transfer resources out of agriculture. . . . New technology will continue to be introduced into farming. The pressures on farm prices and farm incomes will be intolerable unless the income is divided among fewer farm people workers and unless more farms can be organized into economic units with sufficient volume of product to permit use of modern machinery and technology; to allow proper maintenance of the farm itself (the soil, buildings, etc.); and to support the family with a living consistent with American standards. Such an adjustment will strengthen the American system of independent family farms. . . .

For those who want to leave the farm, there is needed vocational guidance, counseling, and training in nonfarm jobs. In addition, direct aid in helping families to move to new locations may be required. . . . In addition to the cash costs, there are adjustments to new schools, churches, and neighborhoods, new kinds of work skills to learn, new friends to make, and other problems. . . .

It is suggested that the Congress authorize a special study by the United States Department of Agriculture of six or eight selected districts comprising several counties each. Such studies should make an inventory of resources, analyze opportunities for self-supporting farming in the area, and determine adjustments needed in farming. They should determine the number of workers who will eventually need to seek employment off the farm, opportunities for off-farm work within the area and in nearby urban areas, and the opportunities for industry to come into the area. . . .

Among the steps that might be necessary are Government purchase or lease of submarginal land for retirement to forest or pasture. Credit and educational programs may be needed for the operators who can develop economic farm units through farm enlargement in some cases and farm development and reorganization in most cases. . . .

For those who stay on the farm in the more serious adjustment areas, increased public investments will be needed in the fields of long-term and intermediate credit for farm enlargement and farm development, and in educational programs to develop farm management know-how.

The Farm Credit Administration and the Farmers Home Administration should test new approaches to improving the quality of credit for those purposes. The greatest deficiency is in the field of intermediate credit. Greater efforts should be made to test programs for cooperation with local banks where the Government underwrites part of the risk. . . .

The pilot studies recommended in this report include:

Production adjustment. Test out a program of land rental to get some crop acres temporarily out of production and into soil-holding crops. Experiment also with longer time rentals of marginal wheat land to get such land into grass permanently.

Moving resources out of agriculture. Find out what kind of aid is needed so that farmers who cannot make a good living on poor farms can make a better living in town. See what kind of help will make better farmers of those who stay in problem areas.

Stimulate consumption of dairy and other livestock products. Test revised food stamp plan in selected areas. Enlarge special school milk and school lunch programs.

Production payment. Use production payments instead of purchase and storage as a way of supporting dairy product prices at 75 per cent of parity. Make use of this experience as a guide if and when support of other livestock or livestock products is considered.

It should be plain that these pilot studies will not provide anything like a complete answer to the major problem of farm production outrunning demand. But they should serve to get farm debate off dead center by directing attention to the major issues and by developing some workable techniques to carry out programs on whose goals there seems to be general agreement.

BIBLIOGRAPHY

An asterisk (*) preceding a reference indicates that the article or a part of it has been reprinted in this book.

BIBLIOGRAPHIES

Cummings, O. comp. Price supports and parity; a selected bibliography. 12p. University of California. Agricultural Experiment Station. Berkeley. '54.

Current History. 27:123-5. F. '54. Recent works on agriculture.

Ulman, Ruth, ed. University debaters' annual: 1949-1950. 335p. H. W. Wilson Co. New York. '50.
    Brannan plan; bibliography. p 130-3.

United States. Department of Agriculture. Low-income farm people: a selected list of references. E. G. Davis, comp. 46p. The Department. Library. Washington 25, D.C. '55.

Wilson Library Bulletin. 28:896-8. Je. '54. Social and economic factors in agriculture; suggested information sources. P. F. Hayes, comp.

BOOKS, PAMPHLETS, AND DOCUMENTS

Aly, Bower, ed. American farm policy: the thirtieth discussion and debate manual. (National University Extension Association. Committee on Debate Materials and Interstate Cooperation. Debate Handbook 30. 1955-1956) 2v. Lucas Brothers. Columbia, Mo. '56.

*American Assembly. United States agriculture: perspectives and prospects; background papers and final report of seventh American Assembly, Harriman, N.Y. May 5-8, '55. 130p. The Assembly. Columbia University. New York 27. '55.
    Reprinted in this book: Johnson, G. L. Agriculture's technological revolution. p27-44; Shepherd, G. S. Surplus disposal and domestic market expansion. p67-78; Jesness, O. B. American agriculture and foreign economic policy. p. 79-88; Penn, R. J. and Loomer, C. W. Conservation of agricultural resources. p 115-22.

Benedict, M. R. Can we solve the farm problem? 601p. Twentieth Century Fund. New York. '56.

Black, J. D. Future food and agriculture policy. McGraw-Hill Book Co. New York. '54.

*Brandt, Karl. Farm price supports—rigid or flexible? (National Economic Problems no452) 18p. American Enterprise Association. 1012 14th St. Washington 5, D.C. '54.

Brandt, Karl. Long range prospects for American agriculture: international trade. 19p. Stanford University Food Research Institute. Stanford, Calif. '53.

Chamber of Commerce of the United States. Information Department. Farm problem. (Information Bulletin no 17) 7p. The Chamber. 1615 H Street. Washington 6, D.C. '54.

*Committee for Economic Development. Research and Policy Committee. Economic policy for American agriculture. 40p. The Committee. 444 Madison Ave. New York 22. '56.

*Conference on Economic Progress. Full prosperity for agriculture. 108p. The Conference. 1001 Connecticut Ave. Washington 6, D.C. '55.

Des Moines Chamber of Commerce. Capital needs of agriculture. 96p. The Chamber. Des Moines 7, Iowa. '53.

Des Moines Chamber of Commerce. Agriculture Department. What price plenty? Proceedings of the 12th annual National Farm Institute, Des Moines, February 17-18, 1950. 118p. The Chamber. Des Moines, Iowa. '50.

Doll, R. J. and Castle, E. N. Financing agriculture through commercial banks. Federal Reserve Bank of Kansas City, Research Department. Kansas City 6, Mo. '52.

Dunbar, R. G. Farmer and the American way. (Oxford Social Studies Pamphlets no 15) 90p. Oxford Book Company. 222 Fourth Ave. New York 3. '52.

*Farm Foundation. Turning the searchlight on farm policy. 82p. The Foundation. 600 S. Michigan Ave. Chicago 5. '52.

Fite, G. C. George N. Peek and the fight for farm parity. 303p. University of Oklahoma Press. Norman. '54.

Forster, G. W. and Leager, M. C. Elements of agricultural economics. 441p. Prentice-Hall. New York. '50.

Halcrow, H. G. ed. Contemporary readings in agricultural economics. 411p. Prentice-Hall. New York. '55.

Hathaway, D. E. Effects of agricultural production controls in 1954 on four Michigan farming areas. 9p. Michigan Agricultural Experiment Station. Michigan State College. East Lansing. '56.

Hibbard, B. H. Agricultural economics. 441p. McGraw-Hill Book Co. New York. '48.

Jesness, O. B. Farm price and income supports. (National Economic Problems Series no437) 29p. American Enterprise Association. 1012 14th St. Washington 5, D.C. '50.

Johnson, V. W. Land problems and policies. 422p. McGraw-Hill Book Co. New York. '54.

Jones, W. O. New agricultural economics. 14p. Stanford University Food Research Institute. Stanford, Calif. '52.

McConnell, Grant. Decline of agrarian democracy. 275p. Iowa State College Press. Ames. '54.

Mighell, R. L. American agriculture: its structure and place in the economy. 187p. Wiley. New York. '55.

National Association of Manufacturers. Research Department. Analysis of the Brannan plan. (Economic Policy Series no 17) 16p. The Association. 2 E. 48th St. New York 17. '49.

*National Farmers Union. Department of Information. What price plenty? 101p. The Union. 1575 Sherman St. Denver, Colo. '54.

National Industrial Conference Board. Prices paid and received by farmers, United States, 1910-1955. The Board. 247 Park Avenue. New York 17. '55.

National Planning Association. Using American agricultural surpluses abroad. Statement by agriculture committee and report by H. R. Tolley. (Pamphlet no91) 30p. The Association. 1606 New Hampshire Ave. Washington 9, D.C. '55.

*National Planning Association. Agriculture Committee on National Policy. New look at farm policy. 42p. The Association. 1606 New Hampshire Ave. Washington 9, D.C. '56.

Newsom, H. D. Task for agriculture. 3p. mimeo. Chamber of Commerce of the United States. Publicity Department. 1615 H St. Washington 6, D.C. '54.

*Poirot, P. L. Agrarian reform. 14p. Foundation for Economic Education. Irvington-on-Hudson, N.Y. '54.

Schikele, Rainer. Agricultural policy. 453p. McGraw-Hill Book Co. New York. '54.

Schultz, T. W. Economic organization of agriculture. 374p. McGraw-Hill Book Co. New York. '54.

Shepherd, G. S. Agricultural price and income policy. 275p. Iowa State College Press. Ames. '54.

Smith, M. G. Fixed and flexible price supports. (Let's Discuss Leaflet no 1) 4p. Ohio State University Agricultural College Extension Service. Columbus. '49.

Smith, M. G. Price supports and income supports. (Let's Discuss Leaflet no2) 4p. Ohio State University Agricultural College Extension Service. Columbus. '49.

Summers, R. E. Subsidies for farmers. (Reference Shelf vol 23 no 1) 208p. H. W. Wilson Co. New York. '52.

Taylor, H. C. and Taylor, A. D. Story of agricultural economics in the United States. 1121p. Iowa State College Press. Ames. '52.

*United States. Commission on Intergovernmental Relations. Study committee report on Federal aid to agriculture. 38p. Supt. of Docs. Washington 25, D.C. '55.

United States. Congress. Program for the low-income population at substandard levels of living; report of the Joint Committee on the Economic Report. 14p. 84th Congress, 2d session. Supt. of Docs. Washington, D.C. '56.

United States. Department of Agriculture. Development of agriculture's human resources; message from the President of the United States; report on problems of low-income farmers. (H. Doc. no 149) 44p. 84th Congress, 1st session. Supt. of Docs. Washington 25, D.C. '55.

*United States. Department of Agriculture. Farmer's share of the consumer's food dollar. K. E. Ogren. (Leaflet no 123) 8p. Supt. of Docs. Washington 25, D.C. '54.

*United States. Department of Agriculture. Price programs. H. S. Henderson and others. (Agriculture Information Bulletin no 135) 107p. The Department. Washington 25, D.C. '53.

United States. Department of Agriculture. Statement by Secretary of Agriculture C. F. Brannan. 7p. The Department. Washington 25, D.C. '49.
> *Reprinted from* Congressional Record. Ap. 7, '49.

United States. Department of Agriculture. Agricultural Marketing Service. Marketing margins for white bread. (Miscellaneous Publication no712) 14p. Supt. of Docs. Washington 25, D.C. '56.

United States. Department of Agriculture. Agricultural Research Service. Agricultural Finance Section, Production Economics Research Branch. Balance sheet of agriculture, 1955. 10p. The Department. Washington 25, D.C. '55.

United States. Department of Agriculture. Bureau of Agricultural Economics. Price spreads between farmers and consumers. R. O. Been. (Agriculture Information Bulletin no4) 95p. Supt. of Docs. Washington 25, D.C. '49.

*United States. Department of Agriculture. Office of the Secretary. Statement by Secretary E. T. Benson before Senate Committee on Agriculture and Forestry, 84th Congress, 2d session, January 12, 1956. 30p. processed. The Department. Washington 25, D.C. '56.

*United States. Department of Agriculture. Office of the Secretary. Talk before National Council of Farmer Cooperatives, Los Angeles, California, January 16, 1956. E. T. Benson. 12p. processed. The Department. '56.

*United States. House of Representatives. Agricultural act of 1956; message from the President of the United States returning without approval the bill (H.R. 12) designated as the "Agricultural act of 1956." (H. Doc. no380) 29p. 84th Congress, 2d session. Supt. of Docs. Washington 25, D.C. '56.
> *Separate:* Text of President's veto message. New York Times. p. 20. Ap. 17, '56.

United States. House of Representatives. Farm relief and agricultural adjustment acts, comp. by E. A. Lewis. 414p. Supt. of Docs. Washington 25, D.C. '50.

United States. House of Representatives. Committee on Agriculture. General farm program; hearings, April 7, 11-12, 25-6, 1949; testimony of Secretary of Agriculture Charles F. Brannan. Part 2. p 138-54. 81st Congress, 1st session. Supt. of Docs. Washington 25, D.C. '49.

United States. House of Representatives. Committee on Agriculture. Long range farm program; hearings April 13, 14, 15, 16, May 5 and 6, 1954; statement of Secretary of Agriculture. E. T. Benson. Part 21. p3977-90. 83d Congress, 2d session. Supt. of Docs. Washington 25, D.C. '54.

United States. Library of Congress. Legislative Reference Service. Alternative policies for American agriculture, by W. W. Wilcox. (Public Affairs Bulletin no67) 29p. Supt. of Docs. Washington 25, D.C. '49.

United States. Library of Congress. Legislative Reference Service. Brannan plan: a proposed farm program. J. K. Rose. (Public Affairs Bulletin no78). 74p. Supt. of Docs. Washington 25, D.C. '50.

United States. Senate. Committee on Agriculture and Forestry. Agricultural act of 1956; report, together with minority views and individual views, February 16, 1956. (S. R. 1484) 71p. 84th Congress, 2d session. Supt. of Docs. Washington 25, D.C. '56.

*United States. Senate. Committee on Agriculture and Forestry. Price support program: hearings, October 23, 1955-January 23, 1956. 8 parts. 3963p. 84th Congress, 2d session. Supt. of Docs. Washington 25, D.C. '56.
    Reprinted in this book: Statement by Ralph S. Bradley. p882-4; Statement by American Farm Bureau Federation. p3515-16; Statement by Herschel D. Newsom. p3521-3; Statement by Melvin F. Gehlbach. p3733-8.

Waite, W. C. and Trelogan, H. C. Introduction to agricultural prices. 227p. Burgess Publishing Co. Minneapolis. '48.

Witt, Lawrence, and Hathaway, D. E. Farmers' plans to change livestock numbers as related to agricultural production controls. 9p. Michigan Agricultural Experiment Station. Michigan State College. East Lansing. '56.

Working, Holbrook. Price supports and the effectiveness of hedging. 8p. Stanford University Food Research Institute. Stanford, Calif. '53.

PERIODICALS

Academy of Political Science Proceedings. 24:78-91. My. '50. Government and agriculture. A. B. Kline.

Agricultural Economics Research. 7:101-7. O. '55. Marketing bill for agricultural products. K. E. Ogren.

Agricultural History. 29:160-9. O. '55. New deal agricultural program and the Constitution. P. L. Murphy.

Agricultural History. 29:174-81. O. '55. Legal parity: implementation of the policy of equality for agriculture, 1929-1954. R. L. Tontz.

Agricultural Situation. 39:3-4. My.; 7-8. Jl. '55. Getting a better understanding about parity prices. R. H. Moats.

Agriculture. 30:6-9. Jl. '55. What about low-income farmers? T. D. Morse.

America. 91:9-11. Ap. 3, '54. Farm price flexibility. P. S. Land.

America. 92:475. F. 5, '55. Farm program for abundance. B. L. Masse. *Discussion*. 93:28. Ap. 2, '55.

America. 93:521-2. S. 3, '55. Secretary Benson and the small farmer.

American Affairs. 12:102-6+. Ap. '50. Story of subsidized agriculture.

American Forum of the Air. 15, no33:1-10. '52. Do we have a sound farm policy? C. F. Brannan and G. D. Aiken.

American Forum of the Air. 16, no36:1-10. S. 6, '53. What's the answer to the farm problem? J. G. Patton and H. D. Newsom.

American Forum of the Air. 17, no9:1-11. Jl. 18, '54. Should Congress adopt the President's farm program? G. D. Aiken and others.

American Magazine. 161:28-9. Ap. '56. What the farmer really wants. Fred Hall.

American Mercury. 82:49-53. Ap. '56. Squeeze on the farmer. A. B. Genung.

Antioch Review. 10:74-83. [Mr.] '50. Bogey in the Brannan plan. R. H. Estabrook.

Atlantic Monthly. 196:13-15. N. '55. Farm prosperity as an issue.

Banking. 48:53+. S. '55. Farm credit and the drop in prices. J. W. Tapp.

Better Farming [*formerly* Country Gentleman]. 125:8+. Je. '55. Farm women tell why we must fight to protect the family farm now. S. J. Knutson.

Better Farming. 125:71+. Je. '55. What ails agriculture. Sally Goldmark.

*Business Week. p23-4. Ap. 2, '55. Answer to the farm problem.

Business Week. p28-9. My. 14, '55. Fewer farmers instead of higher prices.

*Business Week. p 106-26. D. 10, '55. What's behind the new farm crisis.
    Also separate. 11p. Reprint Department. Business Week. 330 W. 42d St. New York 36.

Challenge. p 17-21. My. '55. "Big business" farming. R. L. Holman.

*Christian Century. 72:338. Mr. 16, '55. Surpluses; letter to the editors. J. S. Russell.

Collier's. 131:4-7. Mr. 28, '53. Superfarmer. Henry La Cossitt.

*Collier's. 137:25-7+. Ap. 13, '56. Benson and Brannan debate farm issue. E. T. Benson; C. F. Brannan.

Commercial and Financial Chronicle. 182:969+. S. 8, '55. Nation's farm problem. E. T. Benson.

Commercial and Financial Chronicle. 182:1181+. S. 22, '55. U. S. agriculture and world trade; capacity of farmers to produce has outstripped purchasing power of world consumers; address before International Conference of Agricultural Producers, Rome, September 9, 1955. E. T. Benson.

Commercial and Financial Chronicle. 182:2356+. D. 15, '55. Agriculture; beset with the problems of plenty. L. S. Harden.

Commonweal. 62:71-5. Ap. 22, '55. Trade, aid and the farmer. M. E. Schirber and Emerson Hynes.

*Commonweal. 63:159-61. N. 18, '55. Case for the farmer. James Hearst.

Congressional Digest. 29:71-2. Mr. '50. Farm legislation, 1796-1950.

Congressional Digest. 35:67-96. Mr. '56. New federal plans to aid the farmer; with pro and con discussion.

*Consumer Reports. 14:278-80. Je. '49. Brannan farm plan.

Country Gentleman. 123:36-7+. Ap. '53. He's beating the cost-price squeeze; can you? John Bird.

Country Gentleman. 123:13-14+. O. '53. I believe that a two-price system will give us a better farm program. H. D. Newsom.

Country Gentleman. 123:20+. N. '53. Should we get rid of marginal farms? symposium.

*Country Gentleman. 123:33+. N. '53. Family farm faces a challenge. John Bird.

Country Gentleman. 123:8+. D. '53. I believe high price supports will cost farmers in my state $100,000,000 next year. G. H. Wilson.

Country Gentleman. 124:12+. My. '54. I believe the farmer should get more of the consumer's dollar. K. E. Mundt.

Country Gentleman. 124:136. N. '54. Eisenhower's farm plan.

Country Gentleman. 124:29+. D. '54. Prosperity begins on the farm. C. H. Wilken.

*Current History. 26:91-8. F. '54. Equality for the farmer. G. C. Fite.

*Current History. 26:99-104. F. '54. Farmer's new deal. Theodore Saloutos.

*Current History. 26:105-10. F. '54. Parity and surpluses. Colston Warne.

Current History. 28:321-68. Je. '55. American farm leaders.

*Current History. 28:368-71. Je. '55. Government program for low-income farmers; with presidential covering message. D. D. Eisenhower; E. T. Benson.

Current History. 30:191. Mr. '56. Focus on the American farmer. N. R. Posel.

Democratic Digest. p73-8. Jl. '55. Eisenhower has a "program" but— the small farmer finds the going gets tougher and tougher.

Economist [London]. 157:556-7. S. 10, '49. Puzzle of plenty.

Editorial Research Reports. 2, no22:835-52. D. 7, '49. Brannan plan. W. H. Chartener.

Editorial Research Reports. 2, no 17:749-66. O. 27, '53. Farm price supports. W. F. Dowling.

Editorial Research Reports. 2, no 18:771-87. N. 9, '55. Farm prices and farm income. Martin Packman.

Extension Service Review. 26:9. Ja. '55. Credit, an essential farm tool. R. B. Tootell.

Extension Service Review. 26:131+. Jl. '55. Action program for improving farming in low-income areas. Don Paarlberg.

*Facts Forum. 3:3-7. Ap. '56. Senator Allen J. Ellender, chairman of the Senate committee on agriculture and forestry, reports on the committee's program.

Farm Journal. 74:38-9. F. '50. Can we lick the surpluses? V. Vine and R. D. McMillen.

Farm Journal. 77:23+. O. '53. This two-price plan; with discussion. C. W. Gifford.

Farm Journal. 77:14+. N. '53. Give us high supports. H. M. Simons, Jr.

Farm Journal. 79:35+. Mr. '55. Prosperity: getting your share?

Farm Journal. 79:30-1+. My. '55. Hottest farm argument of the year. H. D. Newsom; E. H. Hill.

Farm Journal. 79:33. Je. '55. Bigger incomes for small farmers.

Farm Journal. 79:37+. N. '55. How bad off are the farmers? C. W. Gifford.

Farm Journal. 79:39+. D. '55. Is the soil bank our next farm program? C. W. Gifford.

Farm Journal. 80:37+. Ja. '56. Farm bureau adopts soil bank. C. W. Gifford.

Farm Journal. 80:14-15+. F. '56. What the farm plan means to you. C. W. Gifford.

Farm Journal. 80:10-11. My. '56. Story behind the President's veto.

Federal Reserve Bulletin. 41:869-78. Ag. '55. Balance sheet of agriculture, 1955.

Foreign Policy Bulletin. 29:2-3. Ap. 14, '50. U.S. farm problem raises baffling trade issues. H. C. Gary.

Foreign Trade. p6-9. My. 15, '55. How the United States government helps the farmer. W. C. Hopper.

Fortune. 41:63-5. Ja. '50. Farmer vs. the people.

Fortune. 41:17-18. F. '50. Farm surpluses.

Fortune. 49:28+. Je. '54. Farmer's money.

Fortune. 51:98-103+. Je. '55. Magnificent decline of U.S. farming. G. H. Burck.
    Reply. Nation. 181:68-9. Jl. 23, '55.

*Fortune. 53:85-6. F. '56. Farm problem: 1956 edition.

Forum. 112:351-63. D. '49. Congress debates: farm price supports.

Harper's Magazine. 211:21-2+. D. '55. Country slickers take us again. John Fischer.
    Discussion. New Republic. 134:14-15. Ja. 9; 7-8. Ja. 30, '56; Harper's Magazine. 212:4+. F. '56.

Journal of Farm Economics. 37:121-5. F. '55. Colin Clark on the future of U.S. agriculture.

Journal of Farm Economics. 37:130-2. F. '55. Proper place of the bigness argument in agricultural economics. C. C. Mitchell.

Journal of Farm Economics. 37:292-3. My. '55. Farm policy; the present position. J. K. Galbraith.

Journal of Farm Economics. 37:353-7. My. '55. Problem of the low-income farmers. J. D. Black.

Journal of Marketing. 19:331-7. Ap. '55. Place of marketing agreements in stabilizing farm income. G. L. Mehren.

Life. 35:40+. N. 9, '53. Benson strikes back at critics. E. T. Benson.

Life. 38:44-8+, 58-9. Ja. 3, '55. Farmer and his government; Bruene family of Iowa; with interview with secretary of agriculture Benson, ed. by Ernest Havemann and D. J. Hamblin. H. F. DeGraff.

Magazine of Wall Street. 96:754-5+. S. 17, '53. Both Republican-Democratic politics prevent farm surplus solution. T. L. Godey.

Nation. 177:231-3. S. 19, '53. Farm bloc and your food dollar. Robert Engler.

Nation's Agriculture. 30:3. Ap. '55. Opportunity unlimited. C. B. Shuman.

Nation's Business. 42:56-7. Ja. '54. Benson seeks a middle course. O. B. Jesness.

*Nation's Busines. 43:56-8. Ja. '55. There's no miracle medicine for farm ills. O. B. Jesness.

*Nation's Business. 43:86-7. F. '55. Food surplus heads overseas. Ben James.

Nation's Business. 43:40-1. Ag. '55. $34 billion farm market is growing. Fred Lindsey.

Nation's Business. 43:42-3+. D. '55. Here's the farm problem. Paul Martin.

Nation's Business. 43:86. D. '55. Look twice at the farmer's plight.

Nation's Business. 44:39-41. Ja. '56. Farmers can prosper and be free. E. T. Benson.

New Republic. 130:9-11. My. 3, '54. Shift to reality must be made. H. A. Wallace.
    Discussion. 130:15-16. My. 10; 30. My. 17; 22-3. My. 31; 30. Je. 14; 131:22-3. Ag. 16, '54.

New Republic. 132:5-6. Ap. 11, '55. Driving the farmer off the land. Tom Fitzsimmons.

New Republic. 133:12-15. D. 19, '55. Farmers' fever chart. Haldore Hansen.

New Republic. 134:16-17. Ja. 16, '56. Agriculture: all the way with Secretary Benson. Leon Keyserling.

New Statesman and Nation. 49:312-14. Mr. 5, '55. Subsidies and farm prices. E. M. H. Lloyd.

New York Times. section IV, p6. N. 13, '55. Arithmetic of the nation's farm problem. E. W. Kenworthy.

New York Times. section IV, p6. Ja. 15, '56. Federal farm policy; present and proposed. W. M. Blair.

*New York Times. section IV, p7. Mr. 11, '56. Parity, basic crops, soil bank, etc.; meanings of terms in the farm bill. W. M. Blair.

New York Times. section III, p 1+. Mr. 25, '56. Lender role dims for U.S. agencies. Paul Heffernan.

*New York Times. p 1+. My. 24, '56. Revised farm bill sent to President. J. D. Morris.

New York Times Magazine. p8. Ja. 28, '51. To stop inflation—starting now. Chester Bowles.

New York Times Magazine. p 12+. Je. 14, '53. Benson: prayer, persuasion and parity. Jay Richter.

New York Times Magazine. p8+. Ag. 1, '54. Farmer looks at farming '54. C. B. Palmer.
    Reply with rejoinder. p. 4. Ag. 29, '54. T. P. Fleming.
New York Times Magazine. p 11+. O. 30, '55. Three farmers look at the farm problem. S. S. King.

New York Times Magazine. p9-11+. Ap. 29, '56. Young farmer faces the farm problem. S. S. King.

Newsweek. 45:26+. Je. 27, '55. Showdown on the plains. R. H. Fleming.

Newsweek. 46:88. O. 24, '55. Farm parity 'fraud.' Henry Hazlitt.

Newsweek. 46:77. O. 31, '55. Farm fiasco: a way out. Henry Hazlitt.

Newsweek. 47:92. F. 6, '56. New acres for old. Raymond Moley.

Progressive. p5-8. Jl.; 11-14. Ag. '55. Crisis on the farm: critical problems of farm and food policy; a package of plenty. R. G. Lewis.

Reader's Digest. 57:63-6. O. '50. Farmer's side of the farm problem. H. D. Cooley.

Reader's Digest. 64:46. My. '54. Heads I lose, tails I lose. S. F. Porter.

Reader's Digest. 67:47-50. Jl. '55. What price too much food? Gaynor Maddox.

Reader's Digest. 68:24-9. Ap. '56. Fantastic farm mess. J. L. Strohm.

Reporter. 2:8-10. Mr. 14, '50. Keeping farmers solvent. Hans Landsburg.

Reporter. 8:21-4. Ap. 14, '53. How fares the land? J. K. Galbraith.

*Reporter. 14:34-7. F. 9, '56. 200 acres in Iowa: 'We need help right now?' Dale Kramer.

Saturday Evening Post. 226:38-9+. My. 15, '54. Just what do these farmers want? John Bird.

Saturday Evening Post. 227:30+. O. 23, '54. Will your grandchildren go hungry? John Bird.

*Saturday Evening Post. 227:30+. Je. 18, '55. Too much is our trouble. Richard Thruelsen.

Saturday Evening Post. 228:38-9+. Ap. 15, '56. How long can we stay on the farm? W. B. Horner.

Saturday Review. 39:22. F. 25, '56. Why the farmer isn't flourishing. R. R. Lord.

Senior Scholastic. 67:12-13+. O. 13, '55. Farmer, political problem child.

Successful Farming. 47:33. N. '49. Let's get straight on price supports, crop controls and nationalization of farmers. E. L. Butz.

Successful Farming. 53:43+. Ap. '55. Let's cut loose from supply and demand. C. C. Mitchell.

Successful Farming. 53:26. Jl. '55. Now, an action-program for low-income farmers. W. E. Swegle.

*Successful Farming. 53:43+. Ag. '55. Agriculture's next big job—make people want farm products. Jim Roe.

Successful Farming. 53:42-3+. O. '55. Here's a different answer to the support problem. J. K. Galbraith.

Successful Farming. 53:38-9. D. '55. Toughest problem in the farm program.

Successful Farming. 54:39+. Ja. '56. How Secretary Benson views to-day's farm problems.

Successful Farming. 54:45+. Ap. '56. Will the soil-bank plan raise your income?

Survey. 86:126-30. Mr. '50. What the farm shooting is all about. Dale Kramer.

Town Meeting (Bulletin of America's Town Meeting of the Air). 15, no48:1-16. Mr. 28, '50. What kind of farm program do we need? Wright Patman and A. B. Kline.

U. S. News & World Report. 35:82-5. O. 2, '53. Here's price squeeze on six million farmers.

U. S. News & World Report. 37:70-2. Jl. 2, '54. There's big money in farming for some.

U. S. News & World Report. 37:77. Jl. 30, '54. We've been asked what parity is all about.

U. S. News & World Report. 37:80-4+. O. 8, '54. Truth about the farm business. E. T. Benson.

U. S. News & World Report. 37:81-2. O. 15, '54. Why farm prices stay high.

U. S. News & World Report. 39:37-9. S. 23, '55. Can a farmer be jailed for planting too much wheat?

U. S. News & World Report. 39:34-6. S. 30, '55. Wanted: a magic formula for the farm problem.

*U. S. News & World Report. 39:30-1. N. 11, '55. What's this "soil bank" idea?

U. S. News & World Report. 39:80-2. D. 30, '55. Not all farmers are in trouble.

U. S. News & World Report. 40:30-2. Ja. 20, '56. Way Ike's farm plan works.

U. S. News & World Report. 40:78-82. Ja. 20, '56. Text of President Eisenhower's message on farm problems sent to Congress January 9, 1956.

U. S. News & World Report. 40:146+. Mr. 16, '56. Are farmers going broke?

U. S. News & World Report. 40:74+. Ap. 27, '56. Ezra Taft Benson: he beat the farm bloc.

U. S. News & World Report. 40:86-7. Ap. 27, '56. How Ike would give the farmers more money.

U. S. News & World Report. 40:109-12. Ap. 27, '56. Why Ike vetoed farm bill: address, April 16, 1956, with excerpts from statement made in the Senate. D. D. Eisenhower.

    Same with title Agricultural Act of 1956. Vital Speeches of the Day. 418:20. My. 1, '56.

U. S. News & World Report. 40:140-2. My. 4, '56. Ike forgot promise to farmers: address, April 23, 1956. L. B. Johnson.

University of Chicago Round Table. 787:1-20. My. 10, '53. Do we have a new farm price policy? J. K. Galbraith and others.

Vital Speeches of the Day. 19:727-31. S. 15, '53. Working together. E. T. Benson.

Vital Speeches of the Day. 22:26-9. O. 15, '55. Address by Ezra Taft Benson, Secretary of Agriculture, before Farm Equipment Institute, New Orleans, Louisiana, September 20, 1955.

Wallaces' Farmer. 80:59. Ag. 6, '55. Too many farmers?

Wallaces' Farmer. 81:6. Ja. 7, '56. Three views on farm aid; Grange, Farm bureau and NFO adopt resolutions recommending action.

Wallaces' Farmer. 81:18. Mr. 3, '56. Fair share for the farmers? Farm Institute speakers debate ways of improving agricultural income.

Wallaces' Farmer. 81:52-3. Mr. 17, '56. Have we a place for them? David Bryant.

Wallaces' Farmer. 81:14. Ap. 21, '56. What the farm bill means to you.

Wallaces' Farmer. 81:38-9. Ap. 21, '56. Will there be surpluses in 1965?